smart clay pot cookery

Carol Heding Munson

Sterling Publishing Co., Inc.
New York

Acknowledgments

A hearty thank you to Russell and Roger, who sampled and critiqued every recipe and enthusiastically offered opinions. And a loving thank you to Lowell for his generous contribution of creative recipes, his cheerful handling of the daily supermarket shuttle, and his invaluable assistance with recipe testing. His encouragement and support made this book possible.

Library of Congress Cataloging-in-Publication Data

Munson, Carol.
    Smart clay pot cookery / Carol Heding Munson.
        p. cm.
    Includes index.
    ISBN 0-8069-7099-5
    1. Clay pot cookery. I. Title.

TX825.5 .M86 2000
641.´89–dc21

                                    00-028506

10 9 8 7 6 5 4 3 2

Published by Sterling Publishing Company, Inc.
387 Park Avenue South, New York, N.Y. 10016
© 2000 by Carol Heding Munson
Distributed in Canada by Sterling Publishing
C/o Canadian Manda Group, One Atlantic Avenue, Suite 105
Toronto, Ontario, Canada M6K 3E7
Distributed in Great Britain and Europe by Chrysalis Books
64 Brewery Road, London N7 9NT, England
Distributed in Australia by Capricorn Link (Australia) Pty Ltd.
P.O. Box 704, Windsor, NSW 2756 Australia

Sterling ISBN 0-8069-7099-5

Contents

Introduction

Bet you just received a clay pot as a gift. How do I know? Well, not so long ago, I, too, was searching shelves in libraries and bookstores for clay pot instructions and recipes. Like you, I'd just been given one as a gift and didn't have a clue about using the thing. What did I find? Not much, so I set about experimenting and devising my own meal-worthy concoctions.

As it turns out, clay pots are marvelous inventions with a long history. They let you whip up intensely flavored roasts and stews, soups, casserole type dishes, puddings, breads, and more, with little attention to the actual cooking. There really isn't much mysterious about them. Basically, it's soak the pot – to create steam – then let everything cook, unattended, in a hot oven.

Because I had so much trouble finding recipes for these low-tech pots, I want to share with you my favorite clay pot creations. These are the ones designed specifically to make the most of the pot's unique talents. You'll find dishes such as Peasant Goulash, Hearty Corn Chowder with Peas, Cheese-Scalloped Potatoes, Chicken Parmesan, Turkey Tetrazzini with Mushrooms, Mediterranean Roast with Eggplant Tarragon Sauce, Cajun Salmon, Cinnamon–Walnut Bread, and Pear–Strawberry Crisp. All are as chic as they are easy. All have a fresh outlook. All are brimming with great taste.

Ready to soak up a pot and cook up a superbly flavored dinner? Me, too. Think I'll go for Pastitsio with Lamb or maybe Basil Meatballs in Red Sauce. Enjoy!

Cooking in a Clay Pot

The culinary world is awash with hot new cooking gadgets, and I love checking out the latest and newest. But the low-tech clay pot isn't among them. Too bad. It's a delightful product. The reason it's missing, however, is understandable: It's been around forever and ever. Fact is, the ancient Romans, famous for their sumptuous feasts, used earthenware pots. Sometimes, simple is best, most enduring, and very ready for a trendy comeback.

Today's pots come in a variety of handy sizes: from small (2- to 5-pound capacity) to large (17-pound capacity). For all-around use, medium is good. It has a 4- to 6-pound capacity, which translates to 3 to 3½ quarts of liquid, the amount the base can hold. Think you might cook fish fairly often? Then look for the shallow fish baker, as well. It's shaped like a fish and quite handsome. Many clay pots feature decorative lids.

Clay pots are available unglazed and glazed. The unglazed variety, which soaks up tons of water, produces plenty of steam for tenderizing meats and vegetables and enhancing flavor. It's an all-purpose pot that's well-suited to cooking roasts and stews and using in a microwave oven.

For baking breads and making pasta casseroles, purists prefer glazed bakeware, which, by the way, has glazing only on the bottom. Glazed pots soak up small amounts of water and produce minimal steam.

GETTING STARTED

Ready to cook in clay bakeware? Or feeling just a trifle intimidated? That's understandable, given the scarcity of instructions and recipes. But take it from me, clay pot cookery is *easy*. It's fun. And cleanup is a snap. But, best of all, the results will wow hungry diners. Let's get started.

Before using your clay pot for the first time, wash it thoroughly with mild dishwashing liquid and warm water. If you want, use a plastic brush to help remove any clay dust residue. Rinse thoroughly, again using warm water.

Next, following the manufacturer's directions, soak the pot and lid in enough cool water to cover for 30 minutes. To save space, invert the lid, and nest the bottom in it. If part of the pot is glazed and part is unglazed, soak only the unglazed portion.

From now on, every time you use your clay pot, soak it – and the lid – for 10 to 15 minutes. Then drain it and wipe out the excess water. Immediately fill the pot with food and place it in the center on the middle rack in a *cold* oven.

HEATING THE OVEN (INCLUDING THE MICROWAVE)

For most recipes and most cookware, preheating the oven is standard procedure. Not so for the clay pot. It's sensitive to heat changes and must be warmed gradually. Here's what to do:

If you have an electric oven, place the pot in the oven while it's still *cold;* then set the oven to the temperature suggested in the recipe. A gas oven, which heats more quickly, must be brought up slowly, so first set the oven to about 200°F (93°C), and let it heat for 5 minutes. Then raise the temperature setting to about 350°F (176.6°C) for 5 minutes. Finally, select the temperature specified in the recipe, usually between 375°F and 500°F (190°C and 260°C).

If you're using a microwave oven, follow the manufacturer's directions. Some microwave manufacturers may recommend using medium or medium-high. A satisfactory starting point, though, is to set the dish on high for 5 minutes. After that, cook the dish on low for approximately 15 minutes for each pound of meat. If the dish is packed with vegetables, especially the longer-cooking root varieties such as carrots, extend the cooking time.

At the end of cooking, expect your clay pot to be *very* hot. Not surprising for foods cooked in a conventional oven – but in the microwave? In this case, yes. That's because the water absorbed during soaking heats up. It, in turn, heats the pot. Be sure to use hot pads (pot holders) when handling a clay pot.

PROTECTING EARTHENWARE

Truth be told, clay pots aren't all that tough. They can and do break, especially when exposed to rapid temperature changes. To protect your pot from cracking, follow these simple guidelines.

*Add cool liquids to cold pots. Warm any liquids destined for hot pots.

*Place your clay pot in a *cold* oven. Never preheat the oven.

6

*Use your clay pot in the oven only, never on the stove top. Direct heat is too intense. To thicken a sauce or make a gravy from pan juices, transfer the liquids to a saucepan.

*Stick to oven use; don't place under the broiler. As with stovetop use, broiler heat is too direct and too intense. That doesn't mean, however, that you must forego nicely browned or crisped foods. For starters, some browning does take place during normal cooking in the clay pot – unless, of course, you're preparing a stew or soup that's brimming with liquid or you're keeping cooking time quite short. For additional browning or crisping, simply remove the lid for the last 5 to 15 minutes of cooking time. At 400°F to 450°F (204°C to 232°C), food will finish up quite nicely. You'll be very pleased with the results, I'm sure.

*Place a hot clay pot on a folded towel or on several cloth pot holders. Otherwise, you risk burning your countertop or, if the surface is cold, breaking the hot pot. After removing the lid, place it on a folded towel as well.

*Use your clay pot for cooking only. It's not designed for storing food in the refrigerator or freezer. Both are way too cold.

*Allow your pot to cool completely before washing it. Cooling may take 30 minutes or so; earthenware retains its heat – a welcome feature when you're using it as a serving vessel.

CLEANING A CLAY POT

For most cooks, kitchen cleanup ranks pretty far down on the pleasure meter. I know; I love cooking, but cleanup ... it's a chore. Fortunately, a clay pot is easy to deal with: Your oven stays clean – no spatters on the walls. And the pot itself comes clean relatively hassle-free. Here are a handful of tips for getting the task done quickly.

*Line the bottom of the pot with parchment paper. The specially treated food-grade paper is nonstick and readily available in almost any large supermarket as well as in cookware shops. The use-and-toss lining will prevent breads, pastas, and other foods from sticking and thus eliminates scrubbing. It will also reduce the absorption of unwanted odors and strong flavors from spices and fish. Who wants tonight's creamy pasta dish to have flavor hints from last night's Creole salmon? Not I, thank you. Don't line the lid. Here, a lining would prevent steaming and would change the fundamental quality of the pot.

*Wash the pot by hand. After the pot cools, wash it with a small amount of dishwashing liquid and rinse it thoroughly under warm water. Never wash it in a dishwasher. The reasons are twofold: Sudden temperature changes might crack the pot. Too much powdered soap can clog the pot's pores and reduce its ability to steam.

*Stay away from scouring powders for the same reason. Bits of powder and other debris can clog the pot's pores. When you need an abrasive cleaner, use ordinary table salt. It works quite well, having just enough grit to get the job done.

*Deodorize with baking soda. Occasionally, fish and strong spices such as curry or cumin will leave a lingering odor in earthenware. To eliminate the unwanted smell, soak the pot bottom and lid for 8 to 10 hours in enough baking-soda solution to cover. For the solution, mix ¼ cup baking soda with a sinkful of water. Then scrub with a plastic brush or plastic scrubbing pad, not a metal one. Rinse thoroughly. An alternate method: Soak the pot for several hours in plain cold water. Drain and fill with cold water and a tablespoon or so of baking soda. Place in a *cold* oven. Set the oven to 450°F (232°C) and cook for 60 minutes. Let cool enough to handle. Scrub and rinse with very hot water. Remember: No sudden temperature changes.

*If earthenware is stored while still damp, it can become moldy. To remove the mold, make a paste of baking soda and water. Then simply spread the paste over the pot. Let dry. Rinse off the paste and dry the pot. This isn't something you'll need to do often − maybe never.

With use, your clay pot will develop a dark patina. That's part of its charm and mystique. Don't try to scrub it away.

STORING EARTHENWARE

Metal and glass saucepans, pots, and bakeware can simply be dried and put away. Earthenware, in my experience, needs a little more attention. First, make certain the pot and lid are thoroughly dry. After washing and towel-drying, let the pot air-dry for at least 24 hours before putting it in a cabinet. Store with the lid inverted in the bottom. That is, avoid closing the pot with the lid in the cooking position. If you have a spare cloth towel, place it between the layers. Because clay needs to breathe, don't store it in a plastic bag.

CONVERTING STANDARD RECIPES

You may wonder if the clay pot is suitable for cooking your favorite standard recipes: casseroles, stews, soups, roasts, and the like. Answer: absolutely. Simply raise the oven temperature by 50°F to 100°F (28°C to 56°C) and increase the cooking time by 10 to 20 minutes. Why the increases? To compensate for two things: the insulating effect of the covered, water-soaked clay pot and the slow start in a cold oven.

BEST BETS

Okay, so now you've read the fundamentals of clay pot cookery. But before you get started, I'd like to share a few hints for recipe success:

*Check for doneness about 10 minutes before a recipe is supposed to be ready. Oven temperatures vary and can speed or slow cooking. (All the recipes in this book were tested in an electric oven.)

*Cut pieces of similar foods into uniform sizes. That way, all the carrots, let's say, in a dish are done at the same time.

*Add peas and other quick-cooking vegetables during the last few minutes of cooking so they don't become overdone.

*Stir in delicate herbs right before serving. High heat and lengthy cooking will diminish their abilities to add pizzazz.

*Trim fat from meats and poultry. That way, the cooking juices will be lean and need little skimming before serving.

CALORIES, FAT, AND OTHER NUTRITIONAL FACTS

Keeping an eagle eye on your intake of calories, fat, sodium, fiber? Then you've come to the right book. I've provided a nutritional breakdown for each recipe. The analyses were done using a computer program called Nutritionist IV by First Data Bank and were calculated for single servings. If you prefer larger or smaller portions, though, you'll be taking in proportionally more or less nutrients.

Special Stews

Veal and Vegetable Stew
with Merlot

Look to turnips for assertive flavor in this earthy dish. It's easy to throw together and sure to satisfy the heartiest of appetites.

Makes 4 servings

2 teaspoons olive oil

1 pound lean veal cubes

¼ teaspoon freshly ground black pepper

1 teaspoon dried oregano

¾ cup fat-free beef broth

½ cup Merlot

4 turnips, cut into ½-inch cubes

12 ounces baby carrots

1 medium onion, thinly sliced

Soak a medium-size clay pot and lid in water for 10 to 15 minutes. While the pot is soaking, warm the oil in a large nonstick skillet over medium heat for 1 minute. Add the veal. Sprinkle the pepper and oregano over the veal. Sauté until lightly browned, 7 to 10 minutes.

Drain the pot and lid. Combine the broth and wine in a 2-cup measure. Pour into the pot. Arrange the veal in bottom of the pot. Top with the turnips, carrots, and onions. Cover the pot, and place in a cold oven. Set oven to 400°F (204°C), and cook for 50 minutes.

Per serving: 283 calories, 6.9 g fat, 160 mg sodium, 5 g dietary fiber.

Quick tip: Any dry red wine can be substituted for the Merlot.

Bratwurst and Sweet Pepper Stew

Take a quick trip to a bier halle *in festive Munich without leaving the familiarity of your kitchen, and savor this sturdy stew. It's brimming with flavorful vegetables and bratwurst, a German pork and veal sausage seasoned with ginger, nutmeg and coriander.*

Makes 4 servings

   1 teaspoon olive oil

   ¼ pound cooked bratwurst, cut in half lengthwise and thickly sliced

   1 large onion, sliced

   3 carrots, sliced diagonally ¾ inch thick

   2 large potatoes, cut into ½-inch cubes

   2 ribs celery, sliced

   1 large red sweet pepper, thinly sliced

   8 cloves garlic, thinly sliced

   1 cup fat-free beef broth

   1 cup nonalcoholic beer

   ¼ teaspoon freshly ground black pepper

   1 teaspoon dried tarragon leaves

Soak a medium-size clay pot and lid in water for 10 to 15 minutes. Meanwhile, warm the oil in a nonstick skillet over medium-high heat for 1 minute. Add the bratwurst and onions, and sauté until the onions are lightly browned, about 8 minutes.

Drain the pot and lid. Transfer the bratwurst mixture to the pot. Add the carrots, potatoes, celery, red peppers, and garlic.

Combine the broth, beer, black pepper, and tarragon leaves in a 2-cup measure. Pour the mixture into the pot. Cover the pot, and place in a cold oven. Set oven to 400°F (204°C), and cook the stew until the vegetables are tender, about 50 minutes.

Per serving: 272 calories, 8.9 g fat, 238 mg sodium, 5.5 g dietary fiber.

Quick tip: If bratwurst is unavailable, substitute kielbasa, a substantial Polish sausage.

Chicken, Carrot, and Apple Stew

At the end of a busy day, enjoy this sensational dish that mixes sweet (apples and raisins) with spicy (curry, turmeric, and hot-pepper sauce).

Makes 4 servings

2 teaspoons olive oil

¾ pound boneless, skinless chicken breast, cut into ¾-inch cubes

1 large onion, cut into thin wedges

1 can (14 ounces) fat-free chicken broth

½ cup dark raisins

2 carrots, sliced ¼-inch thick

1 russet potato, cut into ½-inch cubes

½ cup baby lima beans

1 teaspoon brown sugar

¼ teaspoon celery seeds

½ teaspoon curry powder

⅛ teaspoon ground turmeric

1 Rome apple, chopped

2 tablespoons precooked cornmeal, such as Masarepa®

1 teaspoon Louisiana hot sauce

Soak a medium-size clay pot and lid in water for 10 to 15 minutes. Warm the oil in a large nonstick skillet over medium-high heat for 1 minute. Add the chicken and onions. Cook them until browned, 4 to 6 minutes.

Drain the pot and lid. Transfer the chicken mixture to the pot. Stir in the broth, raisins, carrots, potatoes, lima beans, sugar, celery seeds, curry, turmeric, and apples. Cover the pot, and place in a cold oven. Set oven to 400°F (204°C), and cook until the potatoes are tender, about 1 hour. Stir in the Masarepa and hot sauce.

Per serving: 430 calories, 6.1 g fat, 222 mg sodium, 10.1 g dietary fiber.

Quick tip: Other varieties of apple – Cortland, Empire, Golden Delicious, Granny Smith, Macintosh, and Winesap – can be substituted for the Rome apple.

Chicken with Sun-Dried Tomatoes

Use dry-pack sun-dried tomatoes for intense flavor but no extra fat. The tomatoes are dominant in this recipe, and they provide a surprising hint of sweetness.

Makes 4 servings

- 2 teaspoons olive oil
- ¾ pound boneless, skinless chicken breast, cut into 1-inch cubes
- 1 leek, white part only, thinly sliced
- 2 shallots, chopped
- 1 teaspoon Italian herb seasoning
- 1 large potato, peeled and cubed
- 1 rib celery, sliced
- ½ cup diced sun-dried tomatoes
- 1 cup crushed tomatoes
- 1 cup fat-free chicken broth
- ¼ cup dry red wine
- Parsley sprigs, for garnish

Soak a medium-size clay pot and lid in water for 10 to 15 minutes. While the pot is soaking, warm the oil in a large skillet over medium-high heat for 1 minute. Add the chicken, leeks, shallots and Italian herb seasoning. Sauté, stirring occasionally, until the chicken is lightly browned, 5 to 10 minutes.

Drain the pot and lid. Arrange the potatoes, celery, and sun-dried tomatoes in the pot. Pour in the crushed tomatoes, broth, and wine. Cover the pot, and place in a cold oven. Set oven to 400°F (204°C), and cook for 1 hour. Garnish with the parsley and serve.

Per serving: 308 calories, 5.7 g fat, 419 mg sodium, 3.8 g dietary fiber.

Quick tip: For some recipes, it's important to soak the sun-dried tomatoes before using them. It isn't necessary to do so in this recipe.

Country-Style Chicken Stew Provençal

Rustic stews like this one are loaded with sturdy vegetables and flavorful herbs. Enjoy carrots, potatoes, white beans, and mushrooms steeped in the special flavors of garlic and herbes de Provence.

Makes 4 servings

  2 teaspoons olive oil

  1 pound boneless, skinless chicken breast, cut into 1-inch pieces

  4 ounces portobello mushrooms, cubed

  1 can (14 ounces) fat-free chicken broth

  ¼ cup dry white wine

  4 carrots, thinly sliced

  8 cloves garlic, chopped

  3 medium potatoes, thinly sliced

  1 can (15 ounces) great northern beans, rinsed and drained

  ¼ teaspoon white pepper

  1 teaspoon herbes de Provence

  ¼ cup snipped fresh parsley, for garnish

Soak a medium-size clay pot and lid in water for 10 to 15 minutes. While the pot is soaking, warm the oil in a large nonstick skillet over medium-high heat for 1 minute. Add the chicken and mushrooms, and sauté them until the chicken is lightly browned, about 8 minutes.

Drain the pot and lid. Pour the broth and wine into the pot. Arrange the carrots, garlic, potatoes, and beans in layers in the pot. Sprinkle the pepper over the vegetables. Spread the chicken and mushrooms over the vegetables.

Cover the pot, and place in a cold oven. Set oven to 375°F (190°C), and cook the stew until the chicken is cooked through and the vegetables are tender, 45 to 60 minutes. Season with the herbes. Serve the stew garnished with the parsley.

Per serving: 477 calories, 7.2 g fat, 190 mg sodium, 12 g dietary fiber.

Quick tip: Save time by simply scrubbing, and not peeling, the potatoes.

Grecian Beef Stew

Cinnamon, nutmeg, and lemon give this tomato–beef stew its captivating Greek accent. Serve with a tossed greens salad to make a complete meal.

Makes 4 servings

- 2 teaspoons olive oil
- 1 pound beef rump roast, cut into thin ¾-inch-wide, 2-inch-long strips
- 2 onions, cut into thin wedges
- 1 eggplant (about 12 ounces), peeled and cubed
- 4 cloves garlic, chopped
- Juice of 1 lemon
- 2 cups crushed tomatoes
- ¼ cup dry red wine
- 1 tablespoon brown sugar
- ½ teaspoon ground cinnamon
- ⅛ teaspoon ground nutmeg
- 8 ounces thin egg noodles
- 1 tablespoon crumbled feta cheese, for garnish
- 1 tablespoon chopped fresh mint leaves, for garnish

Soak a medium-size clay pot and lid in water for 10 to 15 minutes. While the pot is soaking, warm the oil in a large skillet over medium-high heat for 1 minute. Add the beef and onions. Sauté until the meat is lightly browned, 6 to 8 minutes.

Drain the clay pot and lid. Combine the meat mixture, eggplant, garlic, lemon juice, tomatoes, wine, sugar, cinnamon, and nutmeg in the pot. Cover the pot, and place in a cold oven. Set oven to 375°F (190°C), and cook for 1½ hours.

While the meat–eggplant mixture is cooking, cook the noodles separately, according to package directions. Drain well. Top noodles with the meat–eggplant mixture when it's done. Garnish each serving with the feta and mint.

Per serving: 520 calories, 8.4 g fat, 386 mg sodium, 7.3 g dietary fiber.

Quick tip: For maximum spicy flavor, use freshly grated nutmeg.

Hickory Steak Stew
with Winter Vegetables

This easy-to-construct stew has an unusual twist: spaghetti squash replaces the more common acorn or butternut variety. Serve with crusty bread to sop up the flavorful broth.

Makes 4 servings

- 1 teaspoon olive oil
- ¾ pound top round beef steak, cut into 1-inch cubes
- 1 large onion, chopped
- 4 cloves garlic, chopped
- 1 can (14 ounces) fat-free beef broth
- ¼ cup hickory-flavored barbecue sauce
- 1 spaghetti squash (about 2 pounds), peeled, seeded, and cut into 2-inch cubes
- 2 parsnips, peeled and sliced
- 2 russet potatoes, peeled and quartered

Soak a medium-size clay pot and lid in water for 10 to 15 minutes. While the pot is soaking, warm the oil in a large nonstick skillet over medium-high heat for 1 minute. Add the beef. Sauté until browned, 5 to 7 minutes. Add the onions and garlic. Sauté just until the onions begin to brown. In a small bowl or 2-cup measure, combine the broth and barbecue sauce.

Drain the pot and lid. Transfer the beef mixture to the pot. Add the squash, parsnips, and potatoes. Pour in the broth. Cover the pot, and place in a cold oven. Set oven to 400°F (204°C), and cook for 1½ hours.

Per serving: 411 calories, 6.9 g fat, 353 mg sodium, 10.6 g dietary fiber.

Quick tip: Use a sturdy chef's knife to peel and chop the spaghetti squash, which has a hard, shell-like skin.

Peasant Goulash

The flavor in this goulash is rich, deep, and complex — thanks to cocoa, tons of paprika, and cooking in a clay pot. This goulash would be equally good over split baked potatoes.

Makes 6 servings

   2 teaspoons olive oil
   1 pound beef rump roast, cut into ½-inch cubes
   4 medium onions, cut into thin wedges
   3 ounces portobello mushrooms, cubed
   1 cup fat-free beef broth
   1 can (14 ounces) stewed tomatoes
   2 cloves garlic, crushed
   1 teaspoon cocoa
   2 tablespoons paprika
   ½ teaspoon marjoram
   ¼ teaspoon freshly ground black pepper
   1 teaspoon browning and seasoning sauce
   8 ounces wide noodles

Soak a medium-size clay pot and lid in water for 10 to 15 minutes. While the pot is soaking, warm the oil in a large nonstick skillet over medium-high heat for 1 minute. Add the beef, onions, and mushrooms. Sauté until lightly browned, 6 to 8 minutes.

Drain the pot and lid. Transfer the beef mixture to the pot. Pour the broth into the skillet. Heat over medium heat, stirring constantly, for 1 to 2 minutes to deglaze the skillet. Pour into the beef mixture. Stir in the tomatoes, garlic, cocoa, paprika, marjoram, and pepper to the pot. Cover the pot, and place in a cold oven. Set oven to 375°F (190°C) and cook for 1 hour 40 minutes.

While the goulash is cooking, cook the noodles according to package directions. Drain thoroughly.

Stir the browning sauce into the goulash. Serve over the noodles.

Per serving: 338 calories, 5.9 g fat, 230 mg sodium, 4.2 g dietary fiber.

Red and White Vegetable Stew with Pork

Simply soul-warming, this easy-to-prepare stew will reward you with complex flavors and heady aromas.

Makes 4 servings

- 1 teaspoon olive oil
- 1 boneless pork chop, trimmed of fat and cut into ½-inch cubes (about 6 ounces)
- 1 medium onion, chopped
- 4 cloves garlic, chopped
- 1 teaspoon cumin seeds
- ¼ teaspoon freshly ground black pepper
- 1 large turnip, chopped
- 1 large russet potato, peeled and cubed
- 2 cups cooked red kidney beans
- 1 can (14 ounces) fat-free chicken broth
- 1 can (8 ounces) no-salt-added tomato sauce
- ½ teaspoon fennel seeds

Soak a medium-size clay pot and lid in water for 10 to 15 minutes. While the pot is soaking, warm the oil in a medium-size skillet for 1 minute. Add the pork, onions, garlic, cumin, and pepper. Sauté until the pork is lightly browned.

Drain the pot and lid. Place the turnips, potatoes, and beans in the pot. Pour in the broth. Top with the pork, tomato sauce, and fennel seeds. Cover the pot, and place in a cold oven. Set oven to 400°F (204°C), and cook for 1 hour.

Per serving: 294 calories, 4.8 g fat, 155 mg sodium, 10 g dietary fiber.

Quick tip: Approximately 2 cups of beans are in a 15-ounce can. If you use the canned variety, be sure to rinse and drain them.

Rustic Chicken Stew with Roasted Peppers

Here's a simple-to-make stew with plenty of home-style flavor from mushrooms, tomatoes, squash, and roasted peppers. A tasty spinoff: Make with cubed pork or turkey breast instead of the chicken.

Makes 4 servings

1 teaspoon olive oil

1 medium onion, sliced

1½ cups sliced mushrooms

1 pound boneless, skinless chicken breast, cut into 1-inch cubes

1 can (14 ounces) sliced stewed tomatoes

3 cups cubed acorn or butternut squash

4 cloves garlic, chopped

2 bay leaves

¼ teaspoon freshly ground black pepper

½ cup chopped roasted red peppers

Soak a medium-size clay pot and lid in water for 10 to 15 minutes. Warm the oil in a large nonstick skillet over medium-high heat for 1 minute. Add the onions, mushrooms, and chicken. Sauté, stirring occasionally, until the chicken is lightly browned, about 8 minutes.

Drain the pot and lid. Transfer the chicken mixture to the pot. Add the tomatoes, squash, garlic, bay leaves, black pepper, and red peppers.

Cover the pot, and place in a cold oven. Set oven to 400°F (204°C), and cook the stew until the chicken is cooked through and the vegetables are tender, about 45 minutes. Discard the bay leaves.

Per serving: 291 calories, 5.5 g fat, 111 mg sodium, 6.8 g dietary fiber.

Quick tip: To save time, use roasted peppers from a jar.

Savory Kielbasa–Potato Stew

This hearty pairing of Polish sausage and red potatoes is low in calories, high in flavor, and will appeal to any appetite. Green peas add a splash of bright color.

Makes 4 servings

½ pound cooked turkey kielbasa, thinly sliced

1 pound red potatoes, diced

1 medium onion, cut into thin wedges

1 rib celery, sliced

2 cups water

2 packets low-sodium beef bouillon powder (or 2 teaspoons bouillon granules)

¼ teaspoon freshly ground black pepper

½ teaspoon dried savory

1 cup frozen peas, thawed

Soak a medium-size clay pot and lid in water for 10 to 15 minutes. Meanwhile, cook the kielbasa in a nonstick skillet over medium-high heat, stirring occasionally, until lightly browned, about 8 minutes.

Drain the pot and lid. Transfer the kielbasa to the pot, and add the potatoes, onions, and celery. Whisk together the water, bouillon, pepper, and savory in a 2-cup measure. Pour the mixture into the pot. Cover the pot, and place in a cold oven. Set oven to 375°F (190°C), and cook the mixture until the vegetables are tender, about 45 minutes.

Stir in the peas, and recover the pot. Cook the stew until the peas are crisp-tender, about 5 minutes.

Per serving: 226 calories, 2.6 g fat, 417 mg sodium, 5.2 g dietary fiber.

Quick tip: Two cups fat-free store-bought beef broth can replace the water and bouillon. Just be aware that the dish will have more sodium.

Super Soups

Cabbage Soup with Walnuts

Dare to be different. Prepare this stylishly simple soup. It has an exceptional yet unique flavor that comes from a combination of bacon, toasted walnuts, and Provolone cheese.

Makes 4 servings

4 slices bacon

2 cans (14 ounces each) fat-free chicken broth

4 cups coarsely chopped green cabbage

1 large onion, chopped

1 carrot, thinly sliced

¼ teaspoon freshly ground black pepper

¼ teaspoon celery seeds

1 cup nonfat sour cream

2 tablespoons chopped walnuts, toasted

2 tablespoons grated Provolone cheese

Soak a medium-size clay pot and lid in water for 10 to 15 minutes. Meanwhile, in a medium-size skillet, cook the bacon over medium heat until crisp. Transfer to a plate lined with paper towels. Crumble.

Drain the pot and lid. Pour the broth into the pot. Add the cabbage, onions, carrots, pepper, celery seeds, and bacon. Cover the pot, and place in a cold oven. Set oven to 425°F (218°C), and cook until the carrots are tender, 45 to 60 minutes.

Stir in the sour cream and walnuts. Garnish each serving with Provolone.

Per serving: 186 calories, 4.6 g fat, 317 mg sodium, 3.4 g dietary fiber.

Quick tip: To toast the walnuts, place them in a small nonstick skillet over low heat. Stir frequently, until slightly browned and fragrant.

Carrot–Fava Bean Soup with Roasted Peppers

This toss-everything-together soup goes together in about 5 minutes so it's perfect for those busy nights when you're feeling too frazzled to fuss over the stove. Fava beans, which have a delightful buttery texture, replace the usual soup beans – red kidney, white, or cannellini.

Makes 4 servings

   2 cans (14 ounces each) fat-free chicken broth

   2 cups cooked and shelled, or rinsed and drained canned fava beans

   2 potatoes, peeled and cubed

   2 carrots, shredded

   ¼ cup chopped roasted red peppers

   ¼ teaspoon freshly ground black pepper

   4 cloves garlic, crushed

Soak a medium-size clay pot and lid in water for 10 to 15 minutes. Drain the pot and lid. Combine the broth, fava beans, potatoes, carrots, red peppers, black pepper, and garlic in the pot. Stir gently to mix. Cover the pot, and place in a cold oven. Set oven to 425°F (218°C), and cook for 1 hour.

Per serving: 240 calories, 0.6 g fat, 362 mg sodium, 7.9 g dietary fiber.

Quick tip: In this recipe, use either roasted red peppers from a jar, or roast your own. For the freshly roasted version, grill or broil a red bell pepper until tender and slightly charred on all sides, 10 to 12 minutes, turning with tongs as needed. Transfer to a glass baking dish with a lid. Close and let steam for 10 minutes. Rub off and discard the charred skin. Quarter and discard the seeds. Chop.

Chorizo–Tortilla Soup

Crisp chips top this zesty, south-of-the-border style soup. Cayenne pepper and chorizo, a Mexican sausage, add the zing while Monterey Jack cheese soothes the bite. Get ready for a superb, palate-stimulating experience.

Makes 4 servings

- 1 teaspoon olive oil
- 2 onions, finely chopped
- 4 cloves garlic, minced
- 1 green bell pepper, finely chopped
- 3 ounces cooked chorizo, thinly sliced
- 3 cups crushed tomatoes
- 1 can (14½ ounces) fat-free chicken broth
- 1 dried cayenne pepper, seeded and minced, or 1 teaspoon crushed red pepper flakes
- 1 teaspoon chopped fresh cilantro
- 6 baked tortilla chips, broken
- ¾ cup (3 ounces) shredded Monterey Jack cheese

Soak a medium-size clay pot and lid in water for 10 to 15 minutes.

Meanwhile, warm the olive oil in a large nonstick skillet over medium-high heat for 1 minute. Add the onions, garlic, bell pepper, and chorizo. Sauté just until the onions turn golden.

Drain the clay pot and lid. Combine the onion mixture, tomatoes, broth, and cayenne pepper or pepper flakes in the pot. Cover the pot, and place in a cold oven. Set oven to 400°F (204°C), and cook for 45 minutes. Stir in the cilantro.

Divide the soup among 4 bowls, and top each serving with the tortilla chips and cheese.

Per serving: 240 calories, 7.2 g fat, 910 mg sodium, 3.2 g dietary fiber.

Quick tip: Toasted flour tortillas or crisp, broken taco shells can replace the tortilla chips.

Creamy Potato Soup

Pleasingly smooth and creamy. Exceptionally easy to make. What more could you ask for in a comforting classic? Great taste. It's here, too.

Makes 4 servings

> 2 cups water
>
> 4 packages low-sodium chicken bouillion
>
> 2 cups cooked or rinsed and drained canned great northern beans
>
> 3 russet potatoes, peeled and chopped
>
> ¼ teaspoon celery seeds
>
> 1 cup shredded cheddar cheese
>
> ½ cup skim milk
>
> Parsley sprigs, for garnish

Soak a medium-size clay pot and lid in water for 10 to 15 minutes. Drain the pot and lid.

Pour the water into the pot. Add the bouillon, beans, potatoes, and celery seeds. Cover the pot, and place in a cold oven. Set oven to 425°F (218°C), and cook for 1 hour.

Mash the potato mixture until smooth, adding the cheese and milk. Garnish with parsley.

Per serving: 311 calories, 0.8 g fat, 232 mg sodium, 8.8 g dietary fiber.

Quick tip: If you prefer a thinner soup, add milk, ¼ cup at a time.

Hearty Corn Chowder with Peas

Thick, flavorful chowders like this one are always a big hit with my family. This potato–corn version gets a spicy kick from Italian sausage and hot pepper sauce.

Makes 4 servings

1 can (14 ounces) low-sodium vegetable broth

2 medium russet potatoes, peeled and cut into ½-inch cubes

2 teaspoons olive oil

2 ounces Italian sausage, chopped into ½-inch cubes

1 large onion, chopped

4 cloves garlic, minced

1 can (15 ounces) cream-style corn

1 cup corn

½ cup peas

1 teaspoon Crystal brand Louisiana-style hot sauce

Soak a medium-size clay pot and lid in water for 10 to 15 minutes. Drain the pot and lid. Add the broth and potatoes to the pot. Cover the pot, and place in a cold oven. Set oven to 425°F (218°C), and cook until the potatoes are tender, about 35 minutes.

Meanwhile, warm the oil in a medium-size skillet over medium-high heat for 1 minute. Add the sausage, onions, and garlic. Sauté until the sausage is lightly brown and the onions are translucent, 5 to 8 minutes.

Transfer half the potatoes to a bowl, and cover with foil to them warm. Mash the potatoes remaining in the pot. Stir in the reserved potatoes, the sausage–onion mixture, the cream-style corn and the corn. Cover the pot and cook for 10 minutes. Stir in the peas and cook until the mixture is hot and bubbly and the peas are tender, about 5 minutes. Stir in the hot sauce.

Per serving: 266 calories, 6.4g fat, 188 mg sodium, 8.3 g dietary fiber.

Quick tip: The intensity of hot sauces varies from mild, such as the Crystal brand used in this recipe, to scorching, such as Tabasco. If using a variety other than Crystal, add a drop at a time and taste-test after each addition.

Italian-Style Tomato Soup

This singular soup gets its rich texture from pureed garbanzo beans and its enticing hint of licorice from fresh basil.

Makes 6 servings

  2 teaspoons olive oil

  1 medium onion, diced

  1 carrot, diced

  1 celery rib, diced

  4 cloves garlic, thinly sliced

  1 can (28 ounces) crushed tomatoes

  1 can (14 ounces) fat-free beef broth

  1 tablespoon red wine vinegar

  1 can (19 ounces) garbanzo beans (chick peas), rinsed, drained, and mashed

  1 tablespoon oregano

  ¼ teaspoon freshly ground black pepper

  6 fresh basil leaves, snipped

Soak a medium-size clay pot and lid in water for 10 to 15 minutes. Meanwhile, warm the oil in a medium-size skillet over medium-high heat for 1 minute. Add the onions, carrots, celery, and garlic, and sauté until the onions are lightly browned.

Drain the clay pot and lid. Combine the tomatoes, broth, vinegar, and beans in the pot. Stir in the oregano, pepper, and basil. Add the onion–carrot mixture. Cover the pot, and place in a cold oven. Set oven to 400°F (204°C), and cook until the vegetables are tender, about 60 minutes.

Per serving: 162 calories, 2.9 g fat, 376 mg sodium, 6.7 g dietary fiber.

Quick tip: To snip the basil quickly, stack the leaves and cut them all at once.

Kielbasa and White Bean Soup

So simple. So tasty. So easy to make that you can whip up this rustic soup for a fuss-free weeknight dinner or fast weekend lunch. Serve with a crusty bread for sopping up the flavorful broth.

Makes 4 servings

  2 ounces cooked kielbasa, thinly sliced

  1 can (14½ ounces) stewed sliced tomatoes

  1 can (14½ ounces) fat-free beef broth

  2 cups cooked or rinsed and drained canned great northern
    beans

  1 large carrot, thinly sliced

  1 potato, chopped

  3 sprigs thyme

  1 tablespoon chili sauce

Soak a medium-size clay pot and lid in water for 10 to 15 minutes. Drain the pot and lid.

Combine the kielbasa, tomatoes, broth, beans, carrots, potatoes, thyme, and chili sauce. Cover the pot, and place in a cold oven. Set oven to 450°F (232°C), and cook for 45 minutes or until carrots and potatoes are tender. Discard the thyme.

Per serving: 225 calories, 1.1 g fat, 381 mg sodium, 8.6 g dietary fiber.

Red Bean and Salami Soup

Just a little salami provides big flavor in this simple soup. I've used red kidney beans, but pinto or a combination of kidney and pinto beans would be equally tasty. If your family and friends are anything like mine, they'll request this basic soup often. But don't tell them how easy it is to toss together.

Makes 6 servings

  2 teaspoons olive oil

  1 small onion, chopped

  6 cloves garlic, chopped

  1 small white eggplant, chopped

  2 cans (14 ounces each) fat-free beef broth

  1 can (15 ounces) diced tomatoes

  1 can (15 ounces) red kidney beans, rinsed and drained

  1 small zucchini, thinly sliced

  2 ounces hard salami, chopped

  ½ teaspoon freshly ground black pepper

  4 sprigs thyme

Soak a medium-size clay pot and lid in water for 10 to 15 minutes. Meanwhile, warm the oil in a large nonstick skillet over medium-high heat for 1 minute. Add the onions, garlic, and eggplant. Sauté, stirring frequently, until the eggplant is lightly browned, about 10 minutes. Add ¼ cup of the broth and stir to deglaze the skillet.

Drain the clay pot and lid. Pour in the eggplant mixture. Add the remaining broth, tomatoes with juice, beans, zucchini, salami, pepper, and thyme.

Cover the pot, and place in a cold oven. Set oven to 400°F (204°C), and cook 60 minutes or until the vegetables are tender. Discard the thyme sprigs.

Per serving: 179 calories, 5.3 g fat, 276 mg sodium, 6.8 g dietary fiber.

Quick tip: If thyme sprigs are young and tender, you can mince them. Sprigs that are woody oldsters should be used whole and discarded after cooking.

Sea Scallop Chowder

Net raves and praise when you make this simply seasoned shellfish soup. If sea scallops aren't available, get bay scallops and shorten the cooking time slightly so these quick-cooking mollusks remain tender and succulent.

Makes 4 servings

  2 potatoes, peeled and thinly sliced

  1 rib celery, thinly sliced

  1 carrot, thinly sliced

  1 onion, thinly sliced and separated into rings

  ½ teaspoon dried thyme leaves

  1 can (10 ounces) clam juice

  ¾ pound sea scallops, cut into uniform-size pieces

  2 ounces cooked lean ham, chopped

  1 cup skim milk, warmed

  2 teaspoons Worcestershire sauce

Soak a medium-size clay pot and lid in water for 10 to 15 minutes. Drain the pot and lid. Place the potatoes, celery, carrots, and onions in the pot. Sprinkle the thyme over the vegetables. Pour in the clam juice.

Cover the pot, and place in a cold oven. Set oven to 400°F (204°C), and cook for 30 minutes. Stir in the scallops and ham. Cook, covered, for another 30 minutes. Stir in the milk and Worcestershire sauce.

Per serving: 237 calories, 2.1 g fat, 622 mg sodium, 3 g dietary fiber.

Quick tip: Two slices of lean, cooked ham from the deli work well in this recipe.

Summer Squash Soup with Watercress

Pale yellow mild squash and deep green peppery-tasting watercress play well together in this light soup. It makes for a delightful first course. Or if soup and sandwiches are to your liking, pair it with seafood salad tucked into pita pocket bread.

Makes 4 servings

- 3 russet potatoes, peeled and chopped
- 1 small yellow squash, thinly sliced
- 2 cans (14 ounces each) fat-free chicken broth
- 4 cloves garlic, crushed
- ½ teaspoon dried marjoram
- ⅛ teaspoon white pepper
- 1 cup watercress

Soak a medium-size clay pot and lid in water for 10 to 15 minutes. Drain the pot and lid. Combine the potatoes, squash, broth, garlic, marjoram, and pepper in the pot. Cover the pot, and place in a cold oven. Set oven to 425°F (218°C) and cook for 45 minutes. Divide the soup among 4 bowls. Top each serving with ¼ cup watercress.

Per serving: 139 calories, 0.3 g fat, 153 mg sodium, 2.7 g dietary fiber.

Quick tip: If you're in a big hurry, you can skip peeling the potatoes. But expect to see flecks of skin floating in the broth.

Turkey–Split Pea Soup

Here's a wonderful home-style soup that'll warm your soul. It takes but minutes to put together; dried split peas are hearty but need no soaking or precooking. I serve it often with a crisp green salad and chewy Russian rye bread.

Makes 4 servings

  1 teaspoon olive oil

  ½ pound turkey breast cutlets, cut into ¾-inch pieces

  1 medium onion, chopped

  2 cans (14 ounces each) fat-free chicken broth

  1 cup water

  ½ cup dried split peas, rinsed and sorted

  1 large potato, peeled and cubed

  1 carrot, thinly sliced

  ½ teaspoon celery seeds

  1 bay leaf

  ⅛ teaspoon white pepper

Soak a medium-size clay pot and lid in water for 10 to 15 minutes. Meanwhile, warm the oil in a large skillet over medium-high heat for 1 minute. Add the turkey and onions. Sauté until lightly browned, about 6 minutes.

Drain the clay pot and lid. Combine the turkey mixture, broth, water, split peas, potatoes, carrots, celery seeds, bay leaf, and white pepper in the pot.

Cover the pot, and place in a cold oven. Set oven to 400°F (204°C), and cook for 1 hour, or until the potatoes are tender. Discard the bay leaf.

Per serving: 260 calories, 2.3 g fat, 230 mg sodium, 9.1 g dietary fiber.

Quick tip: If you can find fresh bay leaves, give them a try. They have far more flavor than the dried variety.

Two-Pepper and Black Bean Soup

Set your palate for an exhilarating experience. This soup is spicy hot and sensational. But you can tame the heat by taking a cue from experienced Mexican cooks: Add a dollop of sour cream to each serving. Of course, you can also turn up the heat. Simply choose a hotter variety of chili pepper.

Makes 6 servings

- 2 cans (14 ounces each) reduced-fat, reduced sodium chicken broth
- 2 russet potatoes, peeled and cubed
- 1 onion, chopped
- 1 cup cooked or rinsed and drained canned black beans
- 2 teaspoons pressed garlic
- 1 rib celery, thinly sliced
- 1 carrot, chopped
- ½ green bell pepper, chopped
- 1 mild chili pepper, seeded and thinly sliced
- 3 ounces cooked sausage, diced
- ½ teaspoon thyme
- ¼ teaspoon freshly ground black pepper
- ½ cup fat-free sour cream

Soak a medium-size clay pot and lid in water for 10 to 15 minutes. Drain the pot and lid. Combine the broth, potatoes, onions, beans, garlic, celery, carrots, bell peppers, chili peppers, sausage, thyme, and black pepper in the pot.

Cover the pot, and place in a cold oven. Set oven to 475°F (246°C), and cook for 45 to 60 minutes, or until the vegetables are tender. Divide the soup among 6 bowls. Top each serving with 1½ tablespoons of the sour cream.

Per serving: 203 calories, 4.3 g fat, 279 mg sodium, 4.8 g dietary fiber.

Quick tip: Wear gloves when seeding and chopping even the mild varieties of chili peppers; the chemical responsible for their culinary heat can sting your fingers.

Vegetable–Rice Soup with Maple Bacon

This superb and classic home-style soup is brimming with green beans and fresh thyme as well as the usual tomatoes and rice. A smidgen of maple-cured bacon adds unforgettable flavor.

Makes 4 servings

- 4 slices maple-cured bacon
- ⅔ cup brown rice
- 2 cans (14 ounces each) fat-free beef broth
- 1 can (14 ounces) diced tomatoes
- 1 cup frozen cut green beans
- 1 medium onion, chopped
- 1 rib celery, thinly sliced
- 3 cloves garlic, chopped
- 1 sprig fresh thyme
- ¼ teaspoon freshly ground black pepper
- ¼ cup snipped fresh dill, for garnish

Soak a medium-size clay pot and lid in water for 10 to 15 minutes. While the pot is soaking, cook the bacon in a nonstick skillet over medium-high heat until it is browned and crisp. Transfer the bacon to a paper-towel-lined plate. Drain the fat from the skillet. Return the skillet to the heat, and add the rice. Cook the rice until it starts to brown, about 10 minutes, shaking the skillet occasionally to "stir" the rice. Crumble the bacon over it.

Pour the broth into the pot. Stir in the rice, tomatoes, beans, onions, celery, garlic, thyme, and pepper. Cover the pot, and place in a cold oven. Set oven to 375°F (190°C), and cook the soup until the rice is tender, about 60 minutes. Stir in the bacon. Serve the soup topped with the dill.

Per serving: 210 calories, 3.5 g fat, 238 mg sodium, 3.5 g dietary fiber.

Quick tip: Cut the dill with scissors, discarding the stem.

Vegetable Soup for All Seasons

Fall, winter, and summer vegetables star in this mostly vegetable soup. If you can't find white turnips, substitute a rutabaga, which some cooks call a swede or Swedish turnip. To make a vegetarian version, replace the chicken broth with vegetable broth.

Makes 8 servings

1 teaspoon olive oil

2 leeks, white part only, thinly sliced

6 cloves garlic, chopped

3 cans (14 ounces each) fat-free chicken broth

3 white potatoes, peeled and cubed

2 white turnips, peeled and shredded

1 small yellow squash, cubed

1 carrot, shredded

2 bay leaves

¼ teaspoon white pepper

1 small green bell pepper, chopped, for garnish

Soak a medium-size clay pot and lid in water for 10 to 15 minutes. Meanwhile, warm the oil in a nonstick skillet over medium-high heat for 1 minute. Add the leeks and garlic; sauté until lightly browned.

Drain the pot and lid. Combine the leek mixture, broth, potatoes, turnips, squash, carrots, bay leaves, and white pepper in the pot. Cover the pot, and place in a cold oven. Set oven to 400°F (204°C), and cook for 1 hour. Discard the bay leaves. Divide the soup among 8 bowls. Garnish each serving with the bell peppers.

Per serving: 130 calories, 0.8 g fat, 133 mg sodium, 3.2 g dietary fiber.

Quick tip: Leeks can be a sandy lot. To clean them, cut off the root ends and trim the tops. Split lengthwise and swish in lots of cold water.

Zucchini–Chicken Soup with Cheddar

When the markets – or your garden – overflow with zucchini and summer squash, here's a deliciously easy way to use some of nature's bounty. Cheddar cheese gives the soup an incomparable richness; garlic and marjoram provide just the right seasoning.

Makes 4 servings

- 2 cans (14 ounces each) fat-free chicken broth
- 2 large russet potatoes, peeled and chopped
- 1 cup water
- 1 medium-size zucchini, shredded
- ½ pound cooked chicken breast, cut into bite-size pieces
- 4 cloves garlic, crushed
- ½ teaspoon dried marjoram leaves
- ⅛ teaspoon white pepper
- 1 cup shredded reduced-fat sharp cheddar cheese
- Oyster crackers (optional)

Soak a medium-size clay pot and lid in water for 10 to 15 minutes. Drain the pot and lid. Add the broth, potatoes, water, zucchini, chicken, garlic, marjoram, and pepper.

Cover the pot, and place in a cold oven. Set oven to 400°F (204°C), and cook until the potatoes are tender, about 1 hour.

Stir in the cheese. Using a hand-held immersion blender, partially puree the mixture. Serve immediately with the crackers, if using.

Per serving: 296 calories, 5.2 g fat, 242 mg sodium, 2.7 g dietary fiber.

Quick tip: About 2 teaspoons crushed garlic from a jar equals 4 garlic cloves.

Mostly Vegetable Entrées and Side Dishes

Baked Shells and Cheese

Here's an updated macaroni and cheese with all the flavor, pizzazz, and comfort of old-fashioned versions. Enjoy often!

Makes 6 servings

- 8 ounces small shell pasta
- 2 cups fat-free milk
- 1 cup shredded extra-sharp cheddar cheese
- 2 tablespoons instant flour
- 1 teaspoon prepared mustard
- 1 teaspoon paprika
- 1 teaspoon Worcestershire sauce
- 1 teaspoon mild pepper sauce
- 2 tablespoons seasoned bread crumbs

Soak a medium-size clay pot and lid in water for 10 to 15 minutes. Meanwhile, cook the pasta according to package directions; drain. Whisk the milk, cheese, flour, mustard, paprika, Worcestershire sauce, and pepper sauce in a medium-size bowl.

Drain the clay pot and lid. Line the pot with parchment paper. Add the pasta. Pour in the milk–cheese mixture. Sprinkle with the bread crumbs.

Cover the pot, and place in a cold oven. Set oven to 375°F (190°C), and cook for 30 minutes. Let stand for 10 minutes before serving.

Per serving: 256 calories, 7 g fat, 184 mg sodium, 1.1 g dietary fiber.

Quick tip: Instant flour blends quickly and easily with liquids for lump-free sauces. If you prefer to use all-purpose flour, whisk thoroughly to eliminate all lumps.

Bayou Beans and Rice

Casual beans and rice have lots of hearty meal appeal in this combine-and-cook dish. It serves 4 as a main dish, or 8 as a side dish.

Makes 4 servings

　1 cup brown rice

　1 can (14 ounces) light red kidney beans, rinsed and drained

　1½ cups fat-free chicken broth

　1 can (14 ounces) sliced stewed tomatoes

　1 onion, chopped

　1 tablespoon mild Louisiana pepper sauce

　½ cup snipped fresh cilantro, for garnish

Soak a medium-size clay pot and lid in water for 10 to 15 minutes. Drain the pot and lid. Combine the rice, beans, broth, tomatoes, onions, and pepper sauce in the pot.

Cover the pot, and place in a cold oven. Set oven to 400°F (204°C), and cook until the rice is tender and the liquid has been absorbed, about 90 minutes. Serve garnished with the cilantro.

Per serving: 358 calories, 1.9 g fat, 298 mg sodium, 9.6 g dietary fiber.

Quick tip: If you use long-grain white rice, reduce the cooking time to about 1 hour.

Cheese-Scalloped Potatoes

Tasters raved, "These are the best scalloped potatoes ever." They're creamy with plenty of rich cheddar flavor, and they're easy enough to serve often. My family adores them. I'm sure yours will, too.

Makes 6 servings

   2 cups 1% milk

   ¼ cup instant flour

   2 teaspoons Dijon mustard

   1 teaspoon Worcestershire sauce

   ¼ teaspoon freshly ground black pepper

   ½ cup shredded sharp cheddar cheese

   4 medium-size russet (Idaho) potatoes (about 2 pounds), thinly sliced

   ½ teaspoon paprika

Soak a medium-size clay pot and lid in water for 10 to 15 minutes. Meanwhile, combine the milk, flour, mustard, Worcestershire sauce, pepper, and cheese in a bowl. Drain the clay pot and lid. Line the pot with parchment paper. Pour in ½ cup of the milk mixture. Arrange the potatoes in thin layers. Pour in the remaining milk mixture. Sprinkle with the paprika.

Cover the pot, and place in a cold oven. Set oven to 400°F (204°C), and cook until the potatoes are tender and most of the liquid has been absorbed, 60 to 75 minutes.

Per serving: 223 calories, 4.3 g fat, 125 mg sodium, 2.9 g dietary fiber.

Quick tip: To save time, don't peel the potatoes, and use a food processor to slice them thinly.

Chili-Stuffed Chayote Squash

Chipotle chili revs up the flavor — and the heat — of the mild, almost bland, chayote squash in this colorful recipe. Serve with sour cream to tame the flame.

Makes 6 servings

- 3 chayote squash, halved
- 1 tamarillo, peeled and sliced
- 1 small onion, quartered
- 4 cloves garlic, halved
- 2 tablespoons minced fresh sage
- 1 chipotle chili, seeded and chopped
- 2 tablespoons recaito sauce
- 1/4 cup water
- 6 sprigs fresh cilantro, chopped
- 6 tablespoons fat-free sour cream

Soak a medium-size clay pot and lid in water for 10 to 15 minutes. Meanwhile, scoop the pulp from the squash, reserving the pulp and leaving 1/8- to 1/4-inch shells. Combine the pulp, tamarillo, onions, garlic, sage, and chipotle in the bowl of a food processor. Process until finely chopped. Stir in the recaito sauce. Spoon into the chayote shells.

Drain the pot and lid. Line the pot with parchment paper. Pour in the water. Arrange the stuffed shells in the pot.

Cover the pot, and place in a cold oven. Set oven to 400°F (204°C), and cook for 60 minutes. Serve with the cilantro and sour cream.

Per serving: 65 calories, 0.3 g fat, 24 mg sodium, 2.4 g dietary fiber.

Quick tips: Chipotle chilies are smoked, dried jalapeño peppers. If you can't find them, substitute another dried hot pepper. Look for recaito sauce, which is similar to sofrito, in the Hispanic section of large supermarkets.

Lasagna Casserole

This vegetarian dish goes together in a flash, courtesy of no-fuss no-boil noodles. I've used crushed tomatoes, which lend a rich tomato flavor. For a lighter sauce, try diced tomatoes.

Makes 6 servings

2 teaspoons olive oil

1 onion, chopped

1 can (28 ounces) crushed tomatoes

1 tablespoon minced fresh basil

2 teaspoons sugar

2 large cloves garlic, crushed

4 to 6 no-boil lasagna noodles

1 cup fat-free ricotta cheese

½ cup shredded mozzarella cheese

2 cups cooked black-eyed peas

¼ cup Parmesan cheese

Soak a medium-size clay pot and lid in water for 10 to 15 minutes. Meanwhile, warm the oil in a medium-size skillet over medium-high heat for 1 minute. Add the onions and sauté for 5 minutes.

Combine the tomatoes, basil, sugar, and garlic in a medium-size bowl.

Drain the pot and lid. Spoon half the tomato mixture into the pot; top with half the noodles, breaking them as necessary to fit. Top with the ricotta, mozzarella, onions, and black-eyed peas. Top with the remaining noodles, the remaining sauce, and the Parmesan.

Cover the pot, and place in a cold oven. Set oven to 425°F (218°C), and cook until the sauce is hot and bubbly and the noodles are al dente, 45 to 60 minutes.

Per serving: 276 calories, 2.1 g fat, 482 mg sodium, 3 g dietary fiber.

Quick tip: To mince basil leaves, stack them; then, starting on a long side, roll up the leaves. Cut crosswise.

Light Baked Beans

Looking for great-tasting beans in a spicy-sweet fresh sauce? End your quest. This recipe fills the bill, without the usual gluey texture. Bonus: These beans keep nicely in the refrigerator for 3 to 4 days, or in the freezer for up to 3 weeks.

Makes 6 servings

> 1 can (14 ounces) diced tomatoes
>
> 1½ cups great northern beans, rinsed and drained
>
> 2 slices bacon, cooked and crumbled
>
> 1 onion, minced
>
> ½ teaspoon crushed garlic
>
> ¼ cup molasses
>
> 1 tablespoon Dijon mustard

Soak a medium-size clay pot and lid in water for 10 to 15 minutes. Drain the pot and lid. Combine the tomatoes with their juice, beans, bacon, onions, garlic, molasses, and mustard in the pot.

Cover the pot, and place in a cold oven. Set oven to 400°F (204°C), and cook for 45 minutes.

Per serving: 126 calories, 1.7 g fat, 60 mg sodium, 4.2 g dietary fiber.

Quick tips: For convenience, use crushed garlic from a jar, and use a food processor to mince the onion.

Orange Rice

Sometimes, low-key is tastiest. This unassuming rice dish gets its special flavor from fresh ginger and grated orange peel.

Makes 4 servings

2 cups fat-free chicken broth

1 cup wild pecan rice

1 tablespoon minced gingerroot

2 teaspoons grated orange peel

Soak a medium-size clay pot and lid in water for 10 to 15 minutes. Drain the pot and lid. Combine the broth, rice, gingerroot, and orange peel in the pot.

Cover the pot, and place in a cold oven. Set oven to 375°F (190°C), and cook until the rice is tender and the liquid has been absorbed, about 45 minutes.

Per serving: 68 calories, 0.1 g fat, 86 mg sodium, 0.3 g dietary fiber.

Quick tip: Other aromatic rices, such as basmati, jasmati, and texmati, can be submitted for the wild pecan rice. Cooking times will be about the same.

Szechuan-Spiced Rice with Chinese Vegetables

Rice is nice with a little spice. Here, Szechuan seasoning – a blend of ginger, black pepper, red pepper, garlic, and paprika – perks up mild-tasting rice. Chinese vegetables add welcome crunch.

Makes 6 servings

 1 can (14 ounces) fat-free chicken broth

 1 cup brown rice

 2 teaspoons reduced-sodium soy sauce

 1 can (8 ounces) sliced water chestnuts, rinsed and drained

 1 can (8 ounces) sliced bamboo shoots, rinsed and drained

 1½ teaspoons Szechuan seasoning

 1 teaspoon crushed garlic

Soak a medium-size clay pot and lid in water for 10 to 15 minutes. Drain the pot and lid. Combine the broth, rice, soy sauce, water chestnuts, bamboo shoots, Szechuan seasoning, and garlic in the pot.

Cover the pot, and place in a cold oven. Set oven to 400°F (204°C), and cook until the rice is tender and the liquid has been absorbed, 60 to 75 minutes.

Per serving: 153 calories, 1.1 g fat, 122 mg sodium, 2.7 g dietary fiber.

Quick tips: If you substitute white rice for the brown variety, reduce the cooking time to about 45 minutes. Other spice blends to try include Thai and Cajun seasonings.

Tomatoes Stuffed with Beans and Rice

In this recipe, juicy ripe tomatoes serve as bowls for a satisfying, creamy filling of refried beans and rice. The flavors – cumin, chili, and peppers – are superbly Southwestern.

Makes 4 servings

4 large tomatoes

½ cup cooked long-grain rice

1 small onion, chopped

½ green bell pepper, chopped

½ cup fat-free refried beans

¼ cup chopped fresh parsley

¼ teaspoon cumin seeds

½ teaspoon chili powder

½ teaspoon crushed red pepper flakes

¼ cup salsa with cheese

Soak a medium-size clay pot and lid in water for 10 to 15 minutes. Slice the tops off the tomatoes. Using a melon baller, scoop out the pulp and place it in a sieve. Using the back of a wooden spoon, press out the juice, discarding it, and chop the tomato pulp.

Place 1 cup of pulp in a medium-size bowl (set the remaining pulp aside for another use). Stir in the rice, onions, peppers, refried beans, parsley, cumin seeds, chili powder, and pepper flakes. Stuff the tomatoes with the mixture. Drain the clay pot and lid. Place the tomatoes in the pot.

Cover the pot, and place in a cold oven. Set oven to 375°F (190°C), and cook for 45 minutes. Top each tomato with 1 tablespoon salsa. Bake, uncovered, for 10 minutes.

Per serving: 155 calories, 2.4 g fat, 486 mg sodium, 5.5 g dietary fiber.

Quick tip: Leave the walls of the tomatoes about ¼-inch thick when removing the pulp; slightly thick walls will help the tomatoes retain their shape during cooking.

Texican Casserole

When you want a hearty vegetarian meal, give this dish a try. It's packed with flavor and overflowing with favorite ingredients: tortillas, tomatoes, salsa, and cheese. And it's guaranteed to win over the taste buds of the entire family — including hard-to-please teens.

Makes 6 servings

  1 onion, chopped

  1 large red bell pepper, chopped

  1 can (15 ounces) diced tomatoes

  1 cup medium-hot salsa

  1 teaspoon minced garlic

  1 teaspoon cumin seeds

  1 can (15 ounces) black beans, rinsed and drained

  1½ cups frozen corn

  2 teaspoons Masarepa® (or other precooked cornmeal)

  1 dried cayenne pepper, seeded and minced

  2 flour tortillas (12-inch)

  ¾ cup shredded Monterey Jack cheese

  1 large tomato, sliced

  4 green or black olives, sliced

  ½ cup fat-free sour cream cheese

Soak a medium-size clay pot and lid in water for 10 to 15 minutes. Meanwhile, combine the onions, bell peppers, cornmeal, diced tomatoes with their juice, salsa, garlic, cumin seeds, beans, corn, and cayenne in a bowl.

Drain the clay pot and lid. Line the pot with parchment paper. Spread one-third of the tomato–bean mixture in the pot. Top with half the tortillas, cutting and overlapping as necessary, and one-third of the cheese. Repeat the layering. Spread the remaining bean mixture over the top. Cover the pot, and place in a cold oven. Set oven to 375°F (190°C), and cook for 1 hour. Top with the remaining cheese and let stand for 10 minutes. Serve topped with the tomato slices, olives, and sour cream.

Per serving: 351 calories, 6.8 g fat, 411 mg sodium, 12.6 g dietary fiber.

Quick tip: Always wear gloves when seeding and mincing hot peppers. The compound responsible for their hot flavor can sting and burn your skin.

Popular Poultry Entrées

Thyme-Honored Chicken

Cooked in a clay pot, poultry is delectably succulent, incredibly tender. But don't just take my word for it. Give this extra-easy roast a shot. You're sure to love the pairing of thyme and apple with chicken.

Makes 6 servings

6-pound oven-roaster chicken

½ teaspoon celery seeds

1 ounce fresh thyme sprigs

1 cup fat-free chicken broth

2 Golden Delicious apples, coarsely sliced

Soak a medium-size clay pot and lid in water for 10 to 15 minutes. Meanwhile, sprinkle the chicken cavity with the celery seeds. Stuff it with half the thyme.

Drain the pot and lid. Pour in the broth. Add the chicken. Arrange the apples and remaining thyme over and around the chicken.

Cover the pot, and place in a cold oven. Set oven to 450°F (232°C), and cook until done throughout and juices run clear (a meat thermometer should register 180°F or 82.2°C), about 2 hours.

Let rest for 15 minutes before carving. Divide the chicken into 3 equal sections. Freeze 2 for later use. Slice the remaining chicken, discarding the skin and thyme sprigs.

Per serving: 140 calories, 4.3 g fat, 76 mg sodium, 1.2 g dietary fiber.

Quick tip: All roasts – turkey, chicken, beef, lamb, pork – are juiciest if you let them rest for 10 to 15 minutes before carving.

Asian Chicken with Basmati Rice

With its high flavor and easy manner, this chicken dish is a certified dinner winner. Basmati rice, a perfumed variety that's popular in Indian cooking, has a light, fluffy texture. For slightly creamy rice, simply cook it as is. For a somewhat dry texture, presoak and rinse the rice to remove exterior starch before cooking.

Makes 6 servings

- 1½ cups basmati rice
- 4 cups fat-free chicken broth
- 2 teaspoons olive oil
- 2 shallots
- 1 rib celery, thinly sliced
- 4 cloves garlic, minced
- 1 tablespoon minced gingerroot
- 1 tablespoon teriyaki sauce
- 3-pound oven-stuffer style chicken

Soak a medium-size clay pot and lid in water for 10 to 15 minutes. Meanwhile, cook the rice in 2½ cups chicken broth according to package directions.

Warm the oil in a small nonstick skillet over medium-high heat for 1 minute. Add the shallots, celery, and garlic. Sauté until tender and golden, about 5 minutes. Stir into the rice. Stir in the gingerroot and teriyaki sauce.

Rinse the chicken, including the cavity, in cold water. Stuff the chicken with the rice mixture; truss, if desired. Drain the pot and lid. Place the chicken in the pot. Pour in the remaining 1½ cups broth.

Cover the pot, and place in a cold oven. Set oven to 450°F (232°C), and cook until the chicken is done throughout (a meat thermometer should register 180°F or 82.2°C), about 1½ hours. Let rest for 10 minutes before carving.

Per serving: 359 calories, 8.4 g fat, 298 mg sodium, 2.2 g dietary fiber.

Quick tip: Extra stuffing can be heated in foil packets in the oven for 30 minutes, or warmed in a microwaveable baking dish, covered, in the microwave on medium-high for 5 minutes.

Caribbean Chicken with Parsnips

This fuss-free dish uses sofrito and lime to give chicken the customary flavors of Caribbean fare. Make your own sofrito – a flavorful concoction of onions, green peppers, garlic, and annatto – or buy ready-made.

Makes 4 servings

2 tablespoons olive oil

2 pounds skinless chicken breasts

2 gloves garlic, chopped

1 pound parsnips, cut into julienne strips

1 pound potatoes, sliced ¼-inch thick

1 can (14 ounces) fat-free chicken broth

¼ cup dry white wine

2 tablespoons sofrito seasoning

1 lime, sliced

¼ cup Masarepa® (or other white precooked cornmeal)

Soak a medium-size clay pot and lid in water for 10 to 15 minutes. Meanwhile, heat the oil in a large skillet over medium-high heat for 1 minute. Add the chicken and garlic. Sauté until the chicken is lightly browned on all sides, about 10 minutes.

Drain the pot and lid. Arrange the vegetables in the pot. Add the chicken, breast side up, and garlic.

Combine the broth, wine, and sofrito in a small bowl. Pour over the chicken. Arrange the lime slices over the chicken. Cover the pot, and place in a cold oven. Set oven to 450°F (232°C), and cook until the chicken is done throughout (a meat thermometer should register 180°F or 82.2°C), about 1 hour and 20 minutes.

Transfer the chicken and vegetables to a platter, reserving the liquid in the pot. Cover the chicken and vegetables with foil to keep warm. Gradually add the Masarepa to the liquid in the clay pot, stirring constantly and vigorously to prevent lumps. Serve over chicken and vegetables.

Per serving: 389 calories, 3.7 g fat, 351 mg sodium, 7.3 g dietary fiber.

Quick tip: Can't find precooked cornmeal at the supermarket? Substitute instant flour; it will dissolve and thicken quickly.

Chicken Parmesan

In this simple dish, the classic duo of tomatoes and cheese takes chicken from ordinary to extraordinary. Mark the recipe for future reference. It's so tasty, you'll have numerous requests to serve it often.

Makes 4 servings

2 teaspoons olive oil

¾ pound skinless, boneless chicken breast

1¼ cups crushed tomatoes

2 large cloves garlic, crushed

1 teaspoon sugar

Pinch of celery seeds

2 tablespoons dry red wine

½ cup shredded mozzarella cheese

2 tablespoons grated Parmesan cheese

Soak a medium-size clay pot and lid in water for 10 to 15 minutes. Meanwhile, warm the oil in a skillet over medium-high heat for 1 minute. Add the chicken and sauté until lightly browned, about 10 minutes.

Drain the clay pot and lid. Combine the tomatoes, garlic, sugar, celery seeds, and wine in the pot. Add the chicken. Combine the cheeses and sprinkle them over the chicken.

Cover the pot, and place in a cold oven. Set oven to 400°F (204°C), and cook until the chicken is cooked through and the cheese melted, about 35 minutes.

Per serving: 249 calories, 8.3 g fat, 364 mg sodium, 1.3 g dietary fiber.

Quick tip: To save time, select store-bought shredded and grated cheeses; but for maximum flavor, choose freshly shredded and grated cheeses.

Creamy Chicken with Roasted Peppers

Here's an updated fast and flavorful version of chicken à la king. If you like, you can stir in ½ cup fresh or frozen peas 5 minutes before cooking is done.

Makes 4 servings

2 teaspoons olive oil

¾ pound chicken, cut into ¾-inch pieces

1 onion, chopped

2 ribs celery, thinly sliced

4 ounces portobello mushrooms, chopped

¾ cup chopped roasted red peppers

1 can (10 ounces) reduced-fat cream of celery soup

¾ cup fat-free milk

¼ cup dry white wine

4 English muffins, split and toasted, or "bake and fill" puff pastry shells

Soak a medium-size clay pot and lid in water for 10 to 15 minutes. Meanwhile, warm the oil in a large skillet over medium-high heat. Add the chicken, onions, celery, and mushrooms. Cook just until the chicken is lightly browned, about 10 minutes.

Drain the pot and lid. Combine the chicken mixture, red peppers, soup (undiluted), milk, and wine in the pot. Cover the pot, and place in a cold oven. Set oven to 400°F (204°C), and cook for 35 minutes.

Serve immediately over the muffins or in the shells.

Per serving: 383 calories, 8 g fat, 613 mg sodium, 5.1 g dietary fiber.

Quick tips: Portobello mushrooms are firmer and meatier than white button mushrooms, but if you can't find the portobello variety, select and slice the everyday white type. Use store-bought roasted red peppers in a jar to save time.

Curried Chicken

Impress a hungry family and guests with this extra-easy, one-pot dish. Turmeric gives it an exotic, deep yellow color, while a foursome of spices – chili powder, curry powder, turmeric, and ginger – provides intriguing savory flavor. It's sure to earn praise from even the pickiest of diners.

3/4-pound skinless, boneless chicken breast, cut into 3/4-inch pieces

2 onions, chopped

4 cloves garlic, minced

1 tablespoon reduced-sodium soy sauce

2 teaspoons chili powder

1 teaspoon curry powder

1 teaspoon turmeric

1 teaspoon powdered ginger

1 teaspoon olive oil

2 cups fat-free chicken broth

1 cup jasmati or other long-grain rice

1/2 cup raisins

1 1/2 cup chopped carrots

Soak a medium-size clay pot and lid in water for 10 to 15 minutes. Drain the pot and lid. Combine the chicken, onions, garlic, soy sauce, chili powder, curry powder, turmeric, ginger, oil, broth, rice, raisins, and carrots in the pot.

Cover the pot, and place in a cold oven. Set oven to 400°F (204°C), and cook for 1 hour.

Per serving: 469 calories, 6.3 g fat, 335 mg sodium, 6.7 g dietary fiber.

Quick tip: Turmeric can stain plastic utensils; use wooden or metal spoons to stir and serve this dish.

Easy Chicken Breasts with Stuffing

Got a hankering for chicken with a traditional bread stuffing but not in the mood to fuss with actually stuffing a chicken? Then give this hassle-free recipe a try. It calls for chicken breasts in lieu of a whole chicken, so you can skip the "stuffing" step. The results are impressive and delicious, I think you'll agree.

Makes 4 servings

- 2 teaspoons olive oil
- 1 rib celery, thinly sliced
- 1 onion, chopped
- 4 ounces portobello mushrooms, chopped
- 2 tablespoons sliced almonds, toasted
- 1²⁄₃ cups chicken broth
- 1 package (6 ounces) stuffing mix with seasoning packet
- ¾ pound skinless, boneless chicken breasts
- 1 teaspoon horseradish mustard

Soak a medium-size clay pot and lid in water for 10 to 15 minutes. Meanwhile, warm the oil in a large skillet over medium-high heat for 1 minute. Add the celery, onions, and mushrooms. Sauté until lightly browned, about 6 minutes. Stir in the almonds, broth, and stuffing mix with seasoning.

Drain the clay pot and lid. Line the pot with parchment paper. Pour the stuffing–mushroom mixture into the pot. Spread the mustard over the chicken. Arrange over the stuffing–mushroom mixture.

Cover the pot, and place in a cold oven. Set oven to 400°F (204°C), and cook for 1 hour. Remove the lid. Cook until the chicken is done throughout and is lightly browned and the liquid has been absorbed, 5 to 10 minutes more.

Per serving: 338 calories, 10 g fat, 371 mg sodium, 3.2 g dietary fiber.

Quick tip: Parchment paper is available in most cookware shops as well as many large supermarkets.

Fennel-Roasted Chicken

A delightful vegetable with a delicate licorice flavor, fennel adds a new dimension to this super-simple dish. Fennel, which has a light green bulb, stalks, and feathery greens, is often mislabeled "sweet anise." Choose crisp bulbs with no browning.

Makes 4 servings

- 1 whole chicken (about 4 pounds)
- ¼ pound fennel root, chopped
- 4 red potatoes, halved
- 4 carrots, cut into 1-inch pieces
- ¼ teaspoon freshly ground black pepper
- 1 cup dry white wine
- Spanish capers, rinsed and drained, for garnish

Soak a medium-size clay pot and lid in water for 10 to 15 minutes. Drain the pot and lid. Place the chicken in the pot. Arrange the vegetables around the sides. Sprinkle with black pepper. Pour in the wine.

Cover the pot, and place in a cold oven. Set oven to 450°F (232°C), and cook until done throughout and juices run clear (a meat thermometer should register 180°F or 82.2°C), about 1½ hours.

Let rest for 10 minutes. Slice and serve garnished with the capers.

Per serving: 400 calories, 4.4 g fat, 141 mg sodium, 5.6 g dietary fiber.

Orange–Basil Chicken with Fruit Salsa

For sensational, refreshing flavor, you can't beat this fruit-and-poultry entrée. If perfect pears aren't available, substitute a red- or green-skinned apple in the salsa. This recipe will charm its way onto your menu often, guaranteed.

Makes 4 servings

    3 pounds chicken breast
    1 orange, thinly sliced
    12 fresh basil leaves
    1 cup fat-free chicken broth
    1 orange, sectioned and diced
    1 pear, diced
    1 shallot, thinly sliced
    1 teaspoon olive oil
    1 tablespoon cider vinegar
    Dash of ground red pepper
    1 teaspoon dry sherry

Soak a medium-size clay pot and lid in water for 10 to 15 minutes. Lift skin on chicken and slide the orange slices and 10 basil leaves under it. Drain the clay pot and lid. Pour broth into pot, and add chicken. Cover the pot, and place in a cold oven. Set oven to 450°F (232°C), and cook until chicken is cooked throughout and juices run clear (a meat thermometer should register 180°F or 82.2°C), 1¼ to 1½ hours.

Meanwhile, mince the remaining 2 basil leaves. Combine the diced orange, pear, shallot, oil, vinegar, red pepper, sherry, and minced basil. Cover and refrigerate until ready to serve.

Divide the chicken into thirds. Freeze two-thirds for later use. Slice the remaining chicken, discarding the skin, oranges, and basil. Serve immediately with the orange–pear mixture.

Per serving: 274 calories, 5.4 g fat, 128 mg sodium, 2.6 g dietary fiber.

Quick tip: The technique of sliding seasonings under poultry skin also works well for whole chickens, turkeys, and Cornish hens.

Swiss–Chicken Casserole

This hearty, home-style dish features tomatoes, pasta, chicken, and cheese. For a quick, complete meal, serve it with your favorite tossed greens salad and a fat-free frozen yogurt for dessert.

Makes 6 servings

   8 ounces rotelle

   2 teaspoons olive oil

   ¾ pound chicken breast, cut into ¾-inch cubes

   4 ounces mushrooms, sliced

   1 can (28 ounces) crushed tomatoes

   4 large cloves garlic, crushed

   12 fresh basil leaves, minced

   1 tablespoon dried minced onions

   2 teaspoons sugar

   ⅛ teaspoon celery seeds

   ⅛ teaspoon freshly ground nutmeg

   1 teaspoon mild pepper sauce

   3 ounces reduced-fat Swiss cheese, cubed

   ¼ cup seasoned bread crumbs

Soak a medium-size clay pot and lid in water for 10 to 15 minutes. Meanwhile, cook the pasta according to package directions. Drain pasta.

Warm the oil in a large skillet over medium-high heat for 1 minute. Add the chicken and mushrooms; sauté until the chicken is lightly browned, 5 to 8 minutes.

Drain the pot and lid. Pour in the tomatoes. Stir in the garlic, basil, onions, sugar, celery seeds, nutmeg, pepper sauce, pasta, chicken and mushrooms, and cheese. Sprinkle the bread crumbs over the pasta–chicken mixture.

Cover the pot, and place in a cold oven. Set oven to 375°F (190°C), and cook for 45 minutes. Uncover and cook for 5 minutes more.

Per serving: 365 calories, 6.5 g fat, 439 mg sodium, 3.6 g dietary fiber.

Quick tip: For maximum flavor, grind your own nutmeg. It's easy to do with either a nutmeg grinder or a simple, sharp hand-held grater.

Balsamic-Seasoned Turkey and Sweet Potatoes

Enjoy a quick Thanksgiving-style dinner year-round. This humble meal of turkey and sweet potatoes goes together in a flash, so you can serve it often. A side of green peas or beans rounds out the meal nicely.

Makes 6 servings

1 can (14 ounces) fat-free chicken broth

1 cup dry white wine

1 tablespoon balsamic vinegar

2 sprigs fresh lemon thyme

4½ pounds turkey breast

1 teaspoon olive oil

½ teaspoon lemon pepper

½ teaspoon fennel seeds

4 sweet potatoes

2 leeks, white part only, sliced

Soak a medium-size clay pot and lid in water for 10 to 15 minutes. Drain the pot and lid. Combine the broth, wine, and vinegar in the pot. Add the lemon thyme and turkey. Rub exposed turkey with the oil; sprinkle with the lemon pepper and fennel. Arrange the potatoes and leeks around the turkey.

Cover the pot, and place in a cold oven. Set oven to 425°F (218°C), and cook until the turkey is done throughout and juices run clear (a meat thermometer should register 180°F or 82.2°C), about 1¾ hours.

Let rest for 10 minutes. Divide the turkey into 6 equal sections. Package and store 5 sections for future use. Slice the remaining part and serve with the potatoes and leeks.

Per serving: 295 calories, 4.1 g fat, 184 mg sodium, 3 g dietary fiber.

Quick tip: Leave the turkey skin in place during cooking to maintain juiciness, but remove it before serving to reduce calories and fat intake.

Easy Turkey Meatballs

Treat yourself – and your family – to flavor-packed meatballs that are right at home over baked potatoes, wide noodles, rice, or pasta. Garnish with paprika and serve with a side of green peas or beans for a complete and very satisfying dinner.

Makes 6 servings

- 1¼ pounds ground turkey breast
- ½ cup quick-cooking oats
- 1 egg white
- 2 tablespoons dried minced onions
- ¼ cup minced fresh parsley
- ½ teaspoon ground nutmeg
- ¼ teaspoon freshly ground black pepper
- 1 teaspoon Worcestershire sauce
- 1 tablespoon olive oil
- 1 cup fat-free chicken broth
- ¼ cup dry white wine
- ¾ cup nonfat sour cream

Soak a medium-size clay pot and lid in water for 10 to 15 minutes. Meanwhile, combine the turkey, oats, egg white, onions, parsley, nutmeg, pepper, and Worcestershire sauce in a large bowl. Mix thoroughly but gently. Shape into 30 walnut-size meatballs.

Warm the oil in a large nonstick skillet over medium-high heat. Add the meatballs. Cook until they're browned on all sides, turning frequently, 8 to 10 minutes.

Drain the pot and lid. Combine the broth and wine in the pot. Add the meatballs. Cover the pot, and place in a cold oven. Set oven to 400°F (204°C), and cook for 45 minutes. Stir in the sour cream. Serve immediately.

Per serving: 226 calories, 3.5 g fat, 132 mg sodium, 1 g dietary fiber.

Quick tip: Form firm meatballs; loose ones will crumble during cooking.

Turkey Tenders with Caper–Madeira Sauce

Looking for an uncommon entrée with fuss-free preparation? Give this one a whirl. The pairing of capers, small, sun-dried flower buds, and Madeira, a fortified Portuguese wine, results in a sauce of complex flavors and subtle richness. The dish is suitable for company but goes together with week-night ease.

Makes 4 servings

- ¼ cup vegetable broth
- 1 onion, finely chopped
- 1 pound turkey tenders
- 1 tablespoon snipped fresh parsley
- 1 teaspoon capers, rinsed and drained
- 2 teaspoons Madeira

Soak a medium-size clay pot and lid in water for 10 to 15 minutes. Drain the pot and lid. Pour in the broth and add the onions. Arrange the turkey in the bottom of the pot. Cover the pot, and place in a cold oven. Set oven to 400°F (204°C), and cook until the turkey is cooked throughout, tender, and juices run clear, 45 to 60 minutes.

Transfer the turkey to a platter and cover with foil to keep warm. Stir the parsley, capers, and Madeira into the liquid remaining in the pot. Slice turkey and spoon sauce over the slices. Serve immediately.

Per serving: 174 calories, 0.9 g fat, 92 mg sodium, 0.7 g dietary fiber.

Quick tip: Capers are packed in a very salty brine. For best flavor, always rinse them before using.

Turkey Tetrazzini with Mushrooms

Cauliflower, mushrooms, and roasted red peppers give this trim Tetrazzini a healthy outlook. And the store-bought condensed soup makes for an easy, success-guaranteed sauce.

Makes 4 servings

   6 ounces spaghetti

   1 tablespoon olive oil

   ¾ pound cooked turkey breast, cut into ½-inch cubes

   1 cup sliced mushrooms

   1 cup small cauliflower florets

   ¼ cup chopped roasted red peppers

   2 tablespoons sliced black olives (4 olives)

   1 cup fat-free chicken broth

   1 can (10¾ ounces) condensed reduced-fat cream of mushroom
      soup

   1 tablespoon dry sherry

   ¼ teaspoon nutmeg

   ½ cup grated hard Provolone cheese

Soak a medium-size clay pot and lid in water for 10 to 15 minutes. Cook the spaghetti in a separate pot according to package; drain.

Warm the oil in a large skillet over medium heat for 1 minute. Add the turkey and mushrooms. Sauté until the mushrooms are lightly browned, about 5 minutes. Combine the spaghetti, turkey, mushrooms, cauliflower, red peppers, and olives in a large bowl. In a medium-size bowl, whisk together the broth, mushroom soup, sherry, and nutmeg. Stir into the turkey mixture.

Drain the clay pot and lid. Line the pot with parchment paper. Pour in the turkey mixture. Sprinkle with the cheese.

Cover the pot, and place in a cold oven. Set oven to 375°F (190°C), and cook until hot and bubbly, 40 to 45 minutes. Let stand for 10 minutes.

Per serving: 426 calories, 10.4 g fat, 487 mg sodium, 2.6 g dietary fiber.

Quick tip: Substitute 1 teaspoon brandy extract for the sherry.

Class-Act Meat Entrées

Corned Beef with Red Cabbage

Corned beef and cabbage, cooked in a clay pot? Absolutely. The meat is deliciously tender and the flavors are superb. Oh, and you don't need to wait until St. Patrick's day to serve this delightful dinner.

Makes 6 servings

1½ pounds corned eye of round beef, trimmed of fat

6½ cups water

4 bay leaves

9 peppercorns

¼ cup red wine vinegar

6 russet potatoes

6 cups coarsely sliced red cabbage

Soak a medium-size clay pot and lid in water for 10 to 15 minutes. Drain the pot and lid. Place the beef in the pot. Add the water, bay leaves, peppercorns, and vinegar. Arrange the potatoes around the beef.

Cover the pot, and place in a cold oven. Set oven to 425°F (218°C), and cook for 2 hours and 45 minutes. Add the cabbage. Cook until tender, about 15 minutes. Discard the bay leaves.

Per serving: 325 calories, 4.5 g fat, 729 mg sodium, 5.5 g dietary fiber.

Quick tip: Leave a bit of core with each slice or wedge of cabbage so the pieces stay together.

Basil Meatballs in Red Sauce

Generous amounts of basil brighten the flavor of these traditional beef favorites. Serve over spaghetti or in rolls. They'll be an instant hit.

Makes 4 servings

¾ pound ground sirloin

½ cup quick oats

1 teaspoon Italian herb seasoning

¼ cup chopped fresh basil leaves

1 egg white

¼ cup grated Romano cheese

¼ cup unbleached flour

2 tablespoons olive oil

1 can (28 ounces) crushed tomatoes

1 onion, chopped

4 cloves garlic, chopped

¼ cup dry red wine

Soak a medium-size clay pot and lid in water for 10 to 15 minutes. Meanwhile, combine the sirloin, oats, Italian seasoning, basil, egg white, and cheese in a large bowl. Form into 1-inch balls and dredge in the flour.

Warm the oil in a large nonstick skillet over medium-high heat for 1 minute. Add the meatballs and cook until browned on all sides, about 10 minutes, turning frequently.

Combine the tomatoes, onions, garlic, and wine in a medium-size bowl. Drain the clay pot and lid. Arrange the meatballs in the pot. Pour in the tomato mixture.

Cover the pot, and place in a cold oven. Set oven to 400°F (204°C), and cook for 45 minutes.

Per serving: 332 calories, 9 g fat, 654 mg sodium, 5.3 g dietary fiber.

Quick tips: Form very firm meatballs and let them cook for several minutes before turning. That way, they won't fall apart.

These meatballs freeze quite nicely for up to a month. So why not double the recipe and freeze half for another day?

Chinese Beef Balls with Bok Choy

These spice-infused meatballs have the power to please your palate. Five-spice powder provides the flavor kick while bok choy, rice sticks, and black bean sauce combine for a stylish accompaniment.

Makes 4 servings

³⁄₄ pound ground sirloin

½ cup quick oats

1 teaspoon five-spice powder

¼ cup chopped bok choy leaves

1 egg white

1 tablespoon dried minced onions

2 teaspoons olive oil

1 can (14 ounces) fat-free beef broth

2 tablespoon black bean sauce

3 cups bok choy stalks, sliced

8 ounces rice sticks

Chinese chili sauce with garlic (optional)

Soak a medium-size clay pot and lid in water for 10 to 15 minutes. Meanwhile, combine the sirloin, oats, five-spice powder, bok choy leaves, egg white, and onions in a large bowl. Form mixture into 1-inch beef balls. Warm the oil in a large nonstick skillet over medium-high heat for 1 minute. Add the beef balls. Cook until lightly browned on all sides, turning occasionally.

Drain the pot and lid. Combine the broth and black bean sauce in the pot. Add the beef balls. Cover the pot, and place in a cold oven. Set oven to 400°F (204°C), and cook for 35 minutes. Stir in the bok choy. Cook until tender, about 10 minutes.

On the stove top, cook the rice sticks according to package directions; drain and divide among 4 plates. Spoon the beef mixture over the rice sticks. Serve with the chili sauce if desired.

Per serving: 304 calories, 9.2 g fat, 190 mg sodium, 3.5 g dietary fiber.

Quick tip: Rice sticks – similar to rice noodles except they are about ¼-inch wide – are available in the Asian section of most large supermarkets, as is Chinese black bean sauce.

Classic Meat Loaf with Mushrooms

Comfort food at its very best: an all-beef meat loaf jazzed up with earthy mushrooms and subtly sweet carrots. It's moist, flavorful, and easy to make, I think you'll agree.

Makes 6 servings

1½ pounds ground sirloin

3 egg whites, lightly beaten

½ cup crushed tomatoes

1 small onion, minced

2 cups firm whole wheat bread crumbs

½ cup chopped mushrooms

2 medium-size carrots, shredded

1 tablespoon brown sugar

2 teaspoons reduced-sodium soy sauce

½ sweet red pepper, cut into thin rings

Fresh basil leaves, for garnish

Soak a medium-size clay pot and lid in water for 10 to 15 minutes. Combine the meat, egg whites, tomatoes, onions, bread crumbs, mushrooms, carrots, sugar, and soy sauce in a large bowl. Shape into a loaf.

Drain the clay pot. Line the bottom of the clay pot with parchment paper and transfer the loaf to the pot. Top with the pepper rings. Cover the pot, and place in a cold oven. Set oven to 400°F (204°C), and cook for 45 minutes. Uncover and bake for 15 minutes more. Garnish with the basil.

Per serving: 310 calories, 6.9 g fat, 460 mg sodium, 2.1 g dietary fiber.

Quick tip: Take care not to overwork the meat loaf, or it will have a compact texture.

Easy Pork–Chipotle Chili

Simmer up a hot chili. This one gets most of its heat from a chipotle – a smoked, dried jalapeño. For less warmth, substitute a mild fresh chili, such as a poblano, and reduce the amount of chili powder.

Makes 6 servings

- ¼ pound cooked, shredded pork
- 1 can (28 ounces) crushed tomatoes
- ⅓ cup water
- 1 tablespoon red wine vinegar
- 2 tablespoons chili powder
- 1 teaspoon cumin seeds
- 1 can (14 ounces) small red beans, rinsed and drained
- 1 can (14 ounces) black beans, rinsed and drained
- 1 large yellow bell pepper, chopped
- 2 cubanel peppers, chopped
- 1 large onion, chopped
- 6 cloves garlic, minced
- 1 small chipotle chili
- Fresh cilantro leaves, for garnish

Soak a medium-size clay pot and lid in water for 10 to 15 minutes. Drain the pot and lid. Combine the pork, tomatoes, water, vinegar, chili powder, cumin seeds, red beans, black beans, bell peppers, cubanel peppers, onions, garlic, and chipotle chili.

Cover the pot, and place in a cold oven. Set oven to 400°F (204°C), and cook for 60 minutes. Discard the chipotle chili. Serve garnished with the cilantro.

Per serving: 298 calories, 2.9 g fat, 369 mg sodium, 15.3 g dietary fiber.

Garbanzo Chili with Ham and Peppers

Chase the chills. This stimulating chili makes for a hot, hearty meal anytime. To moderate the heat, use half a cayenne pepper and less chili powder and serve with fat-free sour cream.

Makes 8 servings

1/4 pound thinly sliced tavern ham, chopped

1 can (28 ounces) crushed tomatoes

1 can (15 ounces) garbanzo beans (chick peas), rinsed and drained

1 can (14 ounces) pinto beans, rinsed and drained

1 large onion, chopped

2 green bell peppers, chopped

1/2 cup water

2 tablespoons chili powder

1 tablespoon cider vinegar

1 teaspoon cumin seeds

6 cloves garlic, minced

1 dried cayenne pepper, seeded and minced

1 small avocado, diced, for garnish

Soak a medium-size clay pot and lid in water for 10 to 15 minutes. Drain the pot and lid. Combine the ham, tomatoes, garbanzo beans, pinto beans, onions, bell peppers, water, chili powder, vinegar, cumin seeds, garlic, and cayenne pepper in the pot.

Cover the pot, and place in a cold oven. Set oven to 400°F (204°C), and cook for 60 minutes. Garnish each serving with the avocado.

Per serving: 268 calories, 6.4 g fat, 644 mg sodium, 11.2 g dietary fiber.

Quick tips: Wear gloves when seeding and chopping chilies. The compound responsible for their heat can sting and burn your fingers. Dip cut avocado in lemon or lime juice to slow browning, or oxidation.

German-Style Sauerbraten

Traditional sauerbraten simmers for hours on the stove top. This oven version has been simplified, and features the same great flavors found in classic recipes.

Makes 4 servings

  1 cup fat-free beef broth

  1 large onion, cut into thin wedges

  2 cloves garlic, minced

  1 teaspoon mixed peppercorns (sometimes called *pepper melange*)

  1 tablespoon pickling spice

  1 bay leaf

  2 cups dry red wine

  1 teaspoon coriander seeds

  1 pound beef rump roast, trimmed of fat

  ½ cup gingersnap crumbs (about 12 cookies)

  ½ cup fat-free sour cream

In a medium-size bowl, combine the broth, onions, garlic, peppercorns, pickling spice, bay leaf, wine, and coriander. Add the beef. Marinate, covered, in the refrigerator for 24 hours, turning once or twice.

Soak a medium-size clay pot and lid in water for 10 to 15 minutes. Drain the pot and lid. Transfer the beef and marinade to the pot.

Cover the pot, and place in a cold oven. Set oven to 375°F (190°C), and cook until the meat is tender, about 2 hours.

Pour the broth mixture through a large strainer into a 2-quart saucepan. Discard the spices and onions. Stir in the gingersnaps. Cook, uncovered, over medium heat until thickened. Stir in the sour cream.

Slice the meat and serve topped with the broth mixture.

Per serving: 388 calories, 7.2 g fat, 295 mg sodium, 1.9 g dietary fiber.

Quick tip: Whole peppercorns, whole allspice, and whole mustard seeds can be substituted for the mixed peppercorns and pickling spice.

Hoisin Pork with Bamboo Shoots

Sweet–spicy and reddish brown in color, hoisin sauce brings authentic Chinese flavor to everyday pork. Bamboo shoots give the dish crunch while roasted red peppers provide a splash of color.

Makes 6 servings

 1 pound pork chops, cut into ¾-inch cubes

 1 can (5 ounces) sliced bamboo shoots, rinsed and drained

 2 ribs celery, thinly sliced

 1 small onion, cut into thin wedges

 ½ cup chopped roasted red pepper

 1 cup fat-free beef broth

 1 tablespoon hoisin sauce

 8 ounces rice sticks

Soak a medium-size clay pot and lid in water for 10 to 15 minutes. Drain the pot and lid. Combine the pork, bamboo shoots, celery, onions, red peppers, broth, and hoisin sauce in the pot.

Cover the pot, and place in a cold oven. Set oven to 400°F (204°C), and cook until the pork is tender, about 1 hour.

Meanwhile, cook the rice sticks according to package directions; drain. Add to the pork mixture, tossing to mix well. Serve immediately.

Per serving: 342 calories, 6.5 g fat, 126 mg sodium, 2.9 g dietary fiber.

Quick tips: Select center-cut pork chops; they usually have the least waste and are, therefore, most reasonably priced. Use roasted red peppers from a jar to save time.

Lime–Salsa Pork Chops

In this dynamite dish, the familiar flavors of lime, onions, and tomatoes complement succulent pork while hot, tender potatoes soak up all the intriguing flavors. Serve with a tossed salad or hot green vegetable, and wait for the raves.

Makes 4 servings

- 1 cup low-sodium vegetable juice
- 4 boneless center-cut loin pork chops (about 1 pound), trimmed of fat
- ½ teaspoon lemon pepper
- 1 lime, cut into 8 slices
- 1 medium onion, cut into 8 slices
- 1 cup medium salsa
- 4 sprigs fresh thyme or ½ teaspoon dried
- 4 medium red potatoes, halved

Soak a medium-size clay pot and lid in water for 10 to 15 minutes and drain them. Pour the juice into the pot and arrange the chops in the bottom. Sprinkle lemon pepper over them. Arrange 2 slices of lime and onion on each chop. Top with the salsa and thyme. Arrange the potatoes around the chops.

Cover the pot, and place in a cold oven. Set oven to 400°F (204°C) and cook until the chops are cooked through and the potatoes are tender, about 60 minutes. Discard the thyme sprigs. Serve the chops topped with the lime, onions, and salsa. Top the potatoes with the salsa.

Per serving: 316 calories, 7.5 g fat, 360 mg sodium, 3.6 g dietary fiber.

Mediterranean Roast with Eggplant–Tarragon Sauce

In this family-style recipe, unassuming eggplant and well-loved tomatoes give everyday pot roast a new twist. Serve with crusty Italian bread for sopping up extra sauce; you won't want to miss a drop.

Makes 8 servings

1 pound eggplant, peeled and cut into ½-inch cubes

1 large onion, chopped

1 can (28 ounces) crushed tomatoes

¼ cup dry red wine

1 teaspoon tarragon leaves

¼ teaspoon freshly ground black pepper

2¼-pound bottom round roast, trimmed of fat

Soak a medium-size clay pot and lid in water for 10 to 15 minutes. Meanwhile, coat a nonstick skillet with cooking spray. Warm over medium-high heat for 1 minute. Add the eggplant. Cook, stirring frequently, for 10 minutes. Remove from the heat. Stir in the onions, tomatoes, wine, tarragon, and pepper.

Drain the pot and lid. Place the roast in the pot. Add the eggplant mixture.

Cover the pot, and place in a cold oven. Set oven to 425°F (218°C), and cook until the roast is tender, 2¾ to 3 hours. Slice, and serve topped with the eggplant mixture.

Per serving: 308 calories, 9.6 g fat, 331 mg sodium, 3.7 g dietary fiber.

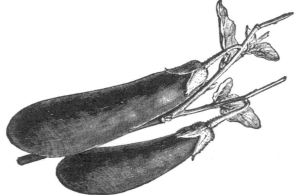

Mustard-Crusted Pot Roast and Potatoes

Here's an updated pot roast with easy preparation and exceptional flavor. Mustard seeds and crushed peppercorns form a pleasing piquant crust; slow-cooking creates a tender roast. This recipe is top notch. Take my word for it!

Makes 8 servings

2¼ cups fat-free beef broth

¼ cup dry red wine

1 small onion, quartered

1 rib celery, quartered

1 small carrot, quartered

1 clove garlic, chopped

1 bay leaf

2½-pound eye of round roast, trimmed of fat

1 teaspoon freshly ground black pepper

2 teaspoons black or yellow mustard seeds

6 potatoes, halved

Soak a medium-size clay pot and lid in water for 10 to 15 minutes. Drain the pot and lid. Combine the broth, wine, onions, celery, carrots, garlic, and bay leaf in the pot. Add the roast. Press the pepper and mustard seeds into the roast above the liquid. Arrange the potatoes around the roast.

Cover the pot, and place in a cold oven. Set oven to 425°F (218°C), and cook until the roast is tender, about 3 hours.

Transfer the meat and potatoes to a serving platter, reserving the liquid. Discard the onion, carrot, celery and bay leaf. Slice the meat. Serve with the potatoes and reserved cooking liquid.

Per serving: 348.9 calories, 7.4 g fat, 146 mg sodium, 2.6 g dietary fiber.

Quick tips: Don't worry if the roast must rest atop chunks of onion and carrot while it cooks. Press the pepper and mustard firmly into the meat.

Pastitsio with Lamb

In this version of pastitsio, a Greek casserole, ricotta cheese replaces the usual white sauce, and crumbled feta is used in lieu of a grated hard cheese. Serve with a light salad of mixed greens and cucumber slices.

Makes 6 servings

8 ounces ziti

1 pound lean ground lamb

1 large onion, chopped

4 cloves garlic, chopped

1/4 teaspoon freshly ground black pepper

1/4 cup dry red wine

2 tablespoons no-salt-added tomato paste

1/2 teaspoon cinnamon

1/2 teaspoon nutmeg

1/2 teaspoon allspice

1 can (28 ounces) plum tomatoes, cut up

1 cup fat-free ricotta cheese

2 ounces feta cheese, crumbled

Olives, for garnish

Cook the ziti according to package directions; drain. Meanwhile, soak a medium-size clay pot and lid in water for 10 to 15 minutes.

Coat a large nonstick skillet with cooking spray. Warm over medium heat for 1 minute. Add the lamb, onions, garlic, and pepper. Cook until the lamb is lightly browned and crumbly, stirring frequently and draining liquid as necessary.

Combine the wine, tomato paste, cinnamon, nutmeg, and allspice in a small bowl. Combine the lamb mixture, plum tomatoes, ricotta cheese, feta cheese, and wine–tomato paste mixture in a large bowl. Drain the clay pot and lid. Line the pot with parchment paper. Pour the lamb mixture into the clay pot. Cover the pot, and place in a cold oven. Set oven to 375°F (190°C), and cook 45 minutes. Uncover and bake for 5 minutes more.

Serve garnished with the olives.

Per serving: 400 calories, 9.4 g fat, 260 mg sodium, 3.5 g dietary fiber.

Pecan-Rubbed Pork

Nuts about nuts? Then sample this pecan-encased pork roast. The meat is succulent; the pecan–mustard top is crisp with a matchless flavor; and the potatoes are infused with a captivating chili broth.

Makes 4 servings

2¼ cups fat-free beef broth

Juice of 1 lemon

2 tablespoons chili sauce

3-pound pork sirloin roast, trimmed of fat

2 tablespoons pecans, ground

1 tablespoon yellow mustard seeds

1 tablespoon brown sugar

1 teaspoon grated lemon peel

¼ teaspoon freshly ground black pepper

4 russet potatoes, halved

Soak a medium-size clay pot and lid in water for 10 to 15 minutes. Drain the pot and lid. Combine the broth, lemon juice, and chili sauce in the pot. Place the roast in the pot.

Combine the pecans, mustard seeds, brown sugar, lemon peel, and pepper in a small bowl; press into the pork above the liquid.

Cover the pot, and place in a cold oven. Set oven to 425°F (218°C), and cook for 1¼ hours. Arrange the potatoes around the roast. Recover, and cook until the pork is done throughout and registers 160°F or 71.1°C on a meat thermometer, 50 to 60 minutes.

Divide the roast into thirds. Freeze two-thirds for later use. Slice the remaining roast and serve with the potatoes.

Per serving: 341 calories, 9.7 g fat, 173 mg sodium, 2.5 g dietary fiber.

Quick tip: Store pecans in a covered container in the freezer, where they'll stay fresh for about a year.

Pineapple Ham

The pairing of ham and pineapple tastes great. A smidgen of horseradish mustard adds zing. Serve with sides of green peas and baked sweet potatoes.

Makes 4 servings

- 2 teaspoons brown sugar
- 2 teaspoons horseradish mustard
- 1 teaspoon dry white wine
- ¾ pound reduced-sodium, fully cooked ham steak
- ½ cup pineapple juice
- 4 to 6 pineapple rings

Soak a medium-size clay pot and lid in water for 10 to 15 minutes. Meanwhile, combine the sugar, mustard, and wine in a small bowl.

Drain the pot and lid. Arrange the ham in the pot. Pour in the pineapple juice. Spread the mustard mixture over the ham. Arrange the pineapple rings atop the ham.

Cover the pot, and place in a cold oven. Set oven to 400°F (204°C), and cook for 40 minutes.

Per serving: 331 calories, 3.5 g fat, 754 mg sodium, 0.3 g dietary fiber.

Quick tip: Use canned sliced pineapple, reserving the juice for the recipe.

Pork Chops Niagara

A New York state wine, with its characteristic subtle Concord grape flavor, makes this a deliciously different entrée. For a complete meal, accompany the dish with a light salad.

Makes 4 servings

- 4 boneless center-cut loin pork chops, sliced ½ inch thick and trimmed of fat (about 1 pound)
- 1 teaspoon olive oil
- 4 cloves garlic, crushed
- ½ teaspoon white pepper
- 1½ cups white wine (for example, New York State Niagara Grape)
- 2 shallots, thinly sliced
- 1 tomato, sliced
- ½ green bell pepper, thinly sliced in rings
- 4 potatoes, quartered

Soak a medium-size clay pot and lid in water for 10 to 15 minutes. Meanwhile, rub the chops with the oil, garlic, and pepper.

Coat a nonstick skillet with cooking spray. Warm for 1 minute. Add the chops and cook until lightly browned on both sides, about 3 minutes a side.

Drain the clay pot and lid. Transfer the chops to the pot. Pour half the wine into the skillet; deglaze. Pour into the pot. Arrange the shallots, tomatoes, and bell peppers over the chops. Arrange the potatoes around the edges of the pot. Pour in the remaining wine.

Cover the pot, and place in a cold oven. Set oven to 425°F (218°C), and cook until the pork is done and the potatoes are tender, about 1 hour. Serve topped with the broth and vegetables.

Per serving: 384 calories, 8.6 g fat, 84 mg sodium, 3.1 g dietary fiber.

Quick tip: To deglaze the skillet, bring the wine to simmering and stir, loosening bits of browned food.

Pork Tenderloin Teriyaki

When you want a pleasant change of pace, here's a dinner of pork and sweet potatoes that can't be ignored. I usually use the large red sweet potatoes, but the smaller yellow-fleshed variety are just as tasty. Serve with peas, green beans, or a tossed salad.

Makes 4 servings

1 tablespoon grated gingerroot

1 teaspoon minced garlic

¼ teaspoon freshly ground black pepper

1 cup fat-free beef broth

1 tablespoon reduced-sodium teriyaki sauce

¾ pound pork tenderloin

1½ pounds sweet potatoes, peeled and quartered

2 onions, cut into wedges

Soak a medium-size clay pot and lid in water for 10 to 15 minutes. Meanwhile, combine the gingerroot, garlic, pepper, and teriyaki in a small bowl. Drain the clay pot and lid. Pour in the broth and add the tenderloin. Rub the top with the teriyaki mixture. Arrange the potatoes and onions around the edges.

Cover the pot, and place in a cold oven. Set oven to 400°F (204°C), and cook until the pork is done throughout and a meat thermometer registers 160°F or 71.1°C, about 1¼ hour. Let rest for 10 minutes.

Per serving: 354 calories, 8.2 g fat, 330 mg sodium, 4.5 g dietary fiber.

Quick tip: Sweet potatoes don't store as well as their white cousins. Keep in a cool dry place, don't refrigerate, and use within a week.

Rich Red Sauce

For pasta lovers: Here's a robust, meaty tomato sauce that will cling beautifully – and tastily – to your favorite pasta, be it spaghetti, fettucine, ziti, or rotelle. A shredded carrot sweetens the sauce, while Provolone cheese boosts flavor and richness.

Makes 6 servings

2 teaspoons olive oil

½ pound ground sirloin

1 onion, chopped

6 cloves garlic, chopped

1 carrot, shredded

¼ cup dry red wine

1 tablespoon no-salt-added tomato paste

½ teaspoon Italian seasoning

¼ teaspoon freshly ground black pepper

1 can (28 ounces) crushed tomatoes

½ cup chopped fresh parsley

½ cup freshly grated Provolone cheese

Soak a medium-size clay pot and lid in water for 10 to 15 minutes. Meanwhile, warm the oil in a large skillet over medium-high heat for 1 minute. Add the sirloin, onions, garlic, and carrots. Sauté until the mixture is lightly browned.

Whisk the wine, tomato paste, Italian seasoning, and pepper in a small bowl. Add to the skillet. Remove from the heat.

Drain the clay pot and lid. Combine the beef mixture and crushed tomatoes in the pot.

Cover the pot, and place in a cold oven. Set oven to 400°F (204°C), and cook for 40 minutes. Stir in the Provolone and parsley. Serve over cooked pasta.

Per serving: 180 calories, 5 g fat, 408 mg sodium, 3.5 g dietary fiber.

Quick tip: Grated Romano or Parmesan cheese can be substituted for the Provolone.

Roast Leg of Lamb Provençal

A sophisticated entrée, this tender leg of lamb begs for inclusion in company-special dinners. Present it with mashed garlic potatoes or a rice pilaf and a green vegetable such as broccoli, asparagus, or peas.

Makes 8 servings

- 1 teaspoon olive oil
- 1 teaspoon herbes de Provence
- 3 pounds lamb shank
- 4 cloves garlic, sliced
- 1 cup fat-free beef broth
- 1 tablespoon dry red wine

Soak a medium-size clay pot and lid in water for 10 to 15 minutes. Meanwhile, combine the oil and herbes de Provence. Cut small slits in the lamb. Stuff with the garlic slices. Rub the herbes de Provence mixture over the lamb.

Drain the clay pot and lid. Line the pot with parchment paper. Pour in the broth and wine. Add the lamb.

Cover the pot, and place in a cold oven. Set oven to 425°F (218°C), and cook until the lamb is done, about 3 hours. Let rest for 10 minutes.

Per serving: 319 calories, 11.9 g fat, 133 mg sodium, 0.1 g dietary fiber.

Quick tip: Use a sharp paring knife to cut the slits in the lamb.

Rosemary Rib Roast

There's nothing timid about a standing rib roast. It's impressive looking and fit for a feast, anytime. Here, you'll be impressed by the marvelous rosemary flavor as well. If you want, substitute russet potatoes for the sweet variety. And be sure to serve a green vegetable or salad.

Makes 8 servings

2¼-pound standing rib roast, bone in

1 teaspoon olive oil

2 teaspoons dried rosemary

½ teaspoon freshly ground black pepper

1 can (14 ounces) fat-free beef broth

1 cup dry red wine (such as Merlot)

8 sweet potatoes (about 3 pounds)

8 ounces crimini mushroom caps, halved

2 teaspoons grated orange peel

Parsley sprigs, for garnish

Soak a medium-size clay pot and lid in water for 10 to 15 minutes. Meanwhile, rub the rib roast with the olive oil, pepper, and rosemary. Warm a large skillet over medium-high heat for 1 minute. Place the roast in the skillet and brown lightly on both sides, about 2 minutes per side.

Drain the clay pot and lid. Pour in the broth and wine. Stand the roast in the pot. Flank it by the potatoes. Add the mushrooms.

Cover the pot, and place in a cold oven. Set oven to 425°F (218°C), and cook until done and a meat thermometer registers at least 145°F (62.8°C), about 1½ hours. Let rest for 10 minutes. Meanwhile, skim fat from the cooking liquid.

Serve with the potatoes and cooking liquid. Sprinkle orange peel over the potatoes before serving. Garnish slices with the parsley.

Per serving: 479 calories, 11.9 g fat, 115 mg sodium, 7.2 g dietary fiber.

Sagely Seasoned Pork Sirloin Roast

Wonderfully subdued and minty, sage keeps this roast moist and flavors it to boot. If you can't find fresh sage, try basil leaves or sprigs of rosemary.

Makes 6 servings

- 2¼ cups fat-free beef broth
- ¼ cup dry white wine
- 1 onion, chopped
- ½ red bell pepper, chopped
- 1 rib celery, chopped
- 1 clove garlic, minced
- 3-pound pork sirloin roast, trimmed of fat
- 2 teaspoons yellow mustard seeds
- 8 to 10 fresh sage leaves
- 1 cup wild pecan rice
- 1 tablespoon pine nuts

Soak a medium-size clay pot and lid in water for 10 to 15 minutes. Drain the pot and lid. Combine broth, wine, onions, peppers, celery, and garlic in the pot. Place the roast in the pot. Press mustard into the roast above the liquid. Arrange the sage over the mustard.

Cover the pot, and place in a cold oven. Set oven to 425°F (218°C), and cook for 1¼ hours. Stir in the rice and nuts. Recover pot. Cook until pork is done and a meat thermometer registers 160°F or 71.1°C, about 45 minutes.

Divide the roast into thirds. Freeze two-thirds for later use. Slice the remaining roast and serve with the rice.

Per serving: 290 calories, 8.4 g fat, 126 mg sodium, 2.6 g dietary fiber.

Quick tip: Look for pine nuts under these names: *pine nuts, Indian nuts, piñon nuts, pignoli,* and *pignolia.*

Savory Lamb Chops

An unusual threesome of mint, chilies, and rosemary jazzes up these lamb chops. The rich, spicy sauce that accompanies the chops is ideal for giving a sprightly twist to potatoes or noodles as well.

1 can (14 ounces) fat-free beef broth

4 sprigs fresh mint

¾ pound lamb shoulder chops, trimmed of fat

2 ounces fresh chives, chopped

2 poblano chilies, seeded and chopped

¼ teaspoon freshly ground black pepper

1 tablespoon fresh rosemary leaves

¼ cup precooked cornmeal (such as Masarepa®) or instant flour

1 teaspoon browning and seasoning sauce

Soak a medium-size clay pot and lid in water for 10 to 15 minutes. Drain the pot and lid. Pour in beef broth. Add the mint. Add the lamb chops and sprinkle with the chives, chilies, black pepper, and rosemary.

Cover the pot, and place in a cold oven. Set oven to 400°F (204°C), and cook until done, about 45 minutes. Transfer the chops to a platter, reserving the cooking liquid, and cover with foil to keep warm. Skim fat from the reserved liquid. Stir in the cornmeal and browning sauce until well combined. Serve over the chops.

Per serving: 237 calories, 10.2 g fat, 134 mg sodium, 1.5 g dietary fiber.

Quick tip: Precooked cornmeal and instant flour dissolve quickly and lump free in hot liquids.

Shredded Beef

Three for one. That's what you'll get when you prepare this tender shredded beef. Cook up the beef, then use it to prepare Beef and Corn Burritos, Spicy Barbecue Beef, and Beef Stir-Fry with Black Bean Sauce.

1 onion, cut into thin wedges

4 cloves garlic, sliced

1 bay leaf

1 tablespoon pickling spice

½ cup cider vinegar

1 teaspoon coriander seeds

2½ cups water

2½ pounds flat beef brisket, trimmed of fat

Soak a medium-size clay pot and lid in water for 10 to 15 minutes. Drain the pot and lid. Combine the onions, garlic, bay leaf, pickling spice, vinegar, coriander seeds, and water in the pot. Add the beef.

Cover the pot, and place in a cold oven. Set oven to 375°F (190°C), and cook very tender, about 3½ hours. Shred the beef, discarding fat. Divide into thirds. Use one-third to make each of the recipes listed above. Discard the cooking liquid and spices.

Spicy Barbecue Beef

Makes 4 servings

1 tablespoon tomato paste

1 cup no-salt-added tomato sauce

3 tablespoons dried minced onions

1 teaspoon olive oil

Juice of ½ lime

1 tablespoon light brown sugar

1 teaspoon horseradish mustard

¼ teaspoon liquid mesquite smoke

About 10 ounces shredded beef brisket (see page 82)

4 Kaiser rolls, split

Combine the tomato paste, tomato sauce, onions, oil, lime juice, brown sugar, mustard, liquid smoke, and beef in a saucepan. Simmer over medium heat until hot throughout, 8 to 10 minutes. Spoon into the rolls.

Per serving: 336 calories, 8.1 g fat, 392 mg sodium, 2.7 g dietary fiber.

Beef Stir-Fry with Black Bean Sauce

Makes 4 servings

    6 ounces Thai rice noodles

    1 tablespoon reduced-sodium soy sauce

    2 tablespoons black bean sauce

    1 tablespoon plus ¾ cup fat-free chicken broth

    2 teaspoons peanut oil

    1 cup thinly sliced red onion wedges

    1 small green bell pepper, cut into thin strips

    About 10 ounces shredded beef brisket (see page 82)

    1 cup coarsely chopped green cabbage, blanched for 1 minute

    1 cup small cauliflower florets, blanched for 1 minute

Cook the noodles according to package directions; drain. Combine the soy sauce, black bean sauce, and 1 tablespoon broth in a small bowl.

Warm the oil in a large nonstick skillet or wok over medium-high heat for 1 minute. Add the onions and peppers. Stir-fry for 2 minutes. Add the beef. Stir-fry for 2 minutes. Add the cabbage and cauliflower. Stir-fry for 2 minutes.

Stir in the soy-sauce mixture. Cover and cook for 2 minutes. Add the noodles, tossing to mix. Pour in the remaining ¾ cup chicken broth. Cover and cook for 1 minute. Serve immediately.

Per serving: 327 calories, 7.3 g fat, 312 mg sodium, 2.5 g dietary fiber.

Southwest Roast Dinner

Better beef. Cumin and mesquite smoke flavor this pot roast and potatoes, instead of the usual celery and black pepper. The meat cooks unattended for several hours until it's fork-tender. It's well worth the wait.

Makes 6 servings

- 1 can (14 ounces) fat-free beef broth
- 1 tablespoon red wine vinegar
- 1 cup water
- 2 pounds bottom round roast, trimmed of fat
- ¼ teaspoon freshly ground black pepper
- 1 teaspoon cumin seeds
- 4 carrots, sliced ½ inch thick
- 2 potatoes, peeled and quartered
- 1 large onion, thickly sliced and separated into rings
- 4 ounces mushroom caps
- 1 teaspoon liquid mesquite smoke

Soak a medium-size clay pot and lid in water for 10 to 15 minutes. Drain the pot and lid. Pour in the broth, vinegar, and water. Add the round roast and season with pepper and cumin seeds. Arrange the carrots, potatoes, onions, and mushrooms, in the order listed, around the roast.

Cover the pot, and place in a cold oven. Set oven to 425°F (218°C), and cook until the meat is tender, about 3 hours. Transfer the roast and vegetables to a serving platter, reserving the liquid. Spoon the liquid smoke over the meat. Cover with foil to keep warm. Let rest for 10 minutes.

Skim the fat from the reserved cooking liquid. Slice the roast. Serve topped with the reserved liquid and accompanied with the vegetables.

Per serving: 376 calories, 7 g fat, 173 mg sodium, 5.2 g dietary fiber.

Spareribs with Sweet–Savory Sauce

Put a new spin on spareribs: Cook them in a clay pot and add a touch of Chinese hoisin sauce to the traditional tomato-based sauce. The results? Delightfully different. Definitely delicious.

Makes 6 servings

SPARERIBS

1 ounce fresh thyme sprigs

2 pounds pork spareribs

4 cups water

1 tablespoon cider vinegar

1 small onion

2 cloves garlic

SWEET–SAVORY SAUCE

2 tablespoons hoisin sauce

1½ cups fat-free beef broth

1 teaspoon celery seeds

2 tablespoons brown sugar

1 tablespoon red wine vinegar

1 tablespoon minced dried onions

½ cup crushed tomatoes

3 tablespoons precooked cornmeal, such as Masarepa

For the spareribs: Soak a medium-size clay pot and lid in water for 10 to 15 minutes. Drain the pot and lid. Line the pot with the thyme. Top with the ribs. Pour in the water and vinegar. Add the onion and garlic.

Cover the pot, and place in a cold oven. Set oven to 400°F (204°C), and cook for 1 hour. Discard the cooking liquid.

For the sauce: Combine the hoisin sauce, broth, celery seeds, brown sugar, vinegar, dried onions, crushed tomatoes, and precooked cornmeal.

Pour sauce over the ribs. Cover the pot. Cook until the pork is done throughout and a meat thermometer registers at least 160°F or 71.1°C, about 60 minutes. Discard the thyme sprigs, whole onion, and whole garlic.

Per serving: 313 calories, 11.7 g fat, 244 mg sodium, 1.1 g dietary fiber.

Quick tip: Purchase ribs that have been cracked for easy serving. And look for country-style ribs; they're meatier than the usual spareribs.

Beef and Corn Burritos

Makes 4 servings

About 10 ounces shredded beef brisket (see page 82)

1 cup frozen corn

1 large tomato, chopped

½ cup medium-hot salsa

1 teaspoon cumin seeds

½ cup chopped roasted red peppers

4 large flour tortillas (10-inch diameter)

¼ cup shredded Monterey Jack cheese

½ cup fat-free sour cream

Preheat oven to 350°F (176.6°C). Combine the beef, corn, tomatoes, salsa, cumin seeds, and red peppers in a saucepan. Cook over medium heat until hot, about 5 minutes.

Spread over the tortillas. Top with the cheese. Roll up. Place, seam side down, in a baking dish. Cover with foil. Heat in the oven until hot throughout, about 5 minutes. Top with sour cream.

Per serving: 329 calories, 8.1 g fat, 372 mg sodium, 4.4 g dietary fiber.

Veal Roast Marsala

A fortified wine hailing from Sicily, Marsala imparts subtle smoky flavor to this potato-and-veal entrée. Complete the meal with a side of lightly steamed peas and carrots. Or try broccoli topped with cheddar cheese.

Makes 4 servings

½ teaspoon ground savory

½ teaspoon marjoram leaves

¼ teaspoon white pepper

1 can (14 ounces) fat-free chicken broth

¼ cup Marsala

2-pound boneless lean round veal roast

Olive-oil spray

4 red potatoes, halved

1 onion, sliced and separated into rings

Soak a medium-size clay pot and lid in water for 10 to 15 minutes. Meanwhile, combine the savory, marjoram, and pepper in a small bowl.

Drain the pot and lid. Pour in the broth and Marsala. Mist the veal with the cooking spray and rub on the savory mixture. Place in the pot and arrange the potatoes around the sides. Top the veal with the onions.

Cover the pot, and place in a cold oven. Set oven to 425°F (218°C), and cook until the veal is done throughout and a meat thermometer registers at least 145°F (62.8°C), about 2 hours. Transfer the roast and potatoes to a platter, reserving the cooking liquid. Cover with foil to keep warm and let rest for 10 minutes. Cut the roast in half. Freeze half for later use. Thinly slice the remaining half. Serve with the potatoes and reserved liquid.

Per serving: 394 calories, 8.1 g fat, 203 mg sodium, 3.5 g dietary fiber.

Catch of the Day
Entrées

Baked Cod with Seasoned Tomatoes

Cod is a white, very mild fish. The slightly assertive flavors of mustard and onion in this recipe give it some welcome pep. My family praises this recipe; I'm sure yours will, too.

Makes 4 servings

1 can (14 ounces) stewed tomatoes

2 teaspoons Worcestershire sauce

1 pound cod

1 teaspoon yellow mustard seeds

1 onion, thinly sliced

1 lemon, sliced

Soak a medium-size clay pot and lid in water for 10 to 15 minutes. Drain the pot and lid. Combine the tomatoes and Worcestershire sauce in the pot. Add the cod. Top with the mustard seeds, onions, and lemon.

Cover the pot, and place in a cold oven. Set oven to 375°F (190°C), and cook until the cod is done and flakes easily when probed with a fork, 50 to 60 minutes.

Per serving: 149 calories, 1.1 g fat, 299 mg sodium, 2.7 g dietary fiber.

Quick tip: Before cooking the cod, use needle-nose pliers to remove fine bones. When the cod is done, it will flake easily and appear opaque from top to bottom.

Cajun Salmon

This special and spicy entrée takes mere minutes to prepare. Serve with baked potatoes and asparagus.

Makes 4 servings

- ½ cup white wine
- 1 pound salmon fillet
- 1 teaspoon olive oil
- 1 teaspoon Cajun seasoning

Soak a medium-size clay pot and lid in water for 10 to 15 minutes. Drain the pot and lid. Line the bottom of the pot with parchment paper. Pour in the wine. Arrange the salmon in the pot. Rub with olive oil and Cajun seasoning.

Cover the pot, and place in a cold oven. Set oven to 400°F (204°C), and cook until the salmon is done throughout and flakes easily when probed with a fork, 30 to 40 minutes.

Per serving: 240 calories, 9.7 g fat, 68 mg sodium, 0.2 g dietary fiber.

Quick tip: Have salmon steaks but no fillet? Follow the same recipe; it'll work just as nicely.

Cod Fillets with Lemon and Thyme

Lemon predominates in this delectable fish dish, which I usually serve with baked potatoes and green peas or a tossed salad. Cod, a lean and firm-fleshed fish, is a close cousin to haddock and pollock.

Makes 4 servings

- ½ cup dry white wine
- 2 bay leaves
- 1 pound cod fillet
- Juice of 1 lemon
- ¼ teaspoon white pepper
- ½ teaspoon thyme leaves
- 1 leek, white part only, sliced
- 4 cloves garlic, minced
- ½ lemon, thinly sliced

Soak a medium-size clay pot and lid in water for 10 to 15 minutes. Drain the pot and lid. Line pot with parchment paper. Pour in the wine and add the bay leaves. Add the cod, skin side down. Pour the lemon juice over the cod. Season with the pepper and thyme. Top with the leeks, garlic, and lemon slices.

Cover the pot, and place in a cold oven. Set oven to 400°F (204°C), and cook until the cod is done throughout and flakes easily when probed with a fork, 30 to 40 minutes. Discard the bay leaves.

Per serving: 170 calories, 1.1 g fat, 97 mg sodium, 1.5 g dietary fiber.

Quick tip: To squeeze the most from a lemon, roll it on a work surface, pressing down firmly, then juice.

Jerk Tilapia Fillets

Popular in Jamaica, jerk seasoning is a spicy blend of dried chilies, thyme, garlic, onions, cinnamon, ginger, allspice, and cloves. It's usually rubbed into pork or chicken before grilling; here it adds zing to a mild, fine-textured fish.

Makes 4 servings

- ½ cup dry white wine
- 1 pound tilapia fillets
- 1 teaspoon olive oil
- 1 teaspoon Caribbean jerk seasoning
- 2 shallots, chopped
- ½ cup chopped fresh parsley
- 1½ pound red potatoes, quartered

Soak a medium-size clay pot and lid in water for 10 to 15 minutes. Drain the pot and lid. Line with parchment paper. Pour in the wine.

Rub the tilapia with the oil and jerk seasoning. Top with the shallots and parsley. Arrange the potatoes around the tilapia.

Cover the pot, and place in a cold oven. Set oven to 400°F (204°C), and cook until the potatoes are tender and the tilapia flakes easily when probed with a fork, about 45 minutes.

Per serving: 292 calories, 4.5 g fat, 75 mg sodium, 2.9 mg dietary fiber.

Quick tip: An easy way to chop parsley is to snip it with sharp kitchen scissors.

Lime Flounder with Mandarin Salsa

Luscious mandarin oranges, lively cilantro, and tangy lime make this refreshing salsa and tropical fish entrée sing. It's elegant enough for company, fast enough for week-night dinners, and it's guaranteed to please.

Makes 4 servings

- ¼ cup white wine
- ¼ cup lime juice
- 1 pound flounder fillets
- Dash white pepper
- ¼ teaspoon ground celery seeds
- 1 shallot, thinly sliced
- ½ cucumber, seeded and diced
- 1 can (11 ounces) mandarin oranges, drained
- 1 tablespoon chopped fresh chives
- 1 teaspoon olive oil
- 1 tablespoon cider vinegar
- Dash of ground red pepper
- 2 teaspoons chopped fresh cilantro

Soak a medium-size clay pot and lid in water for 10 to 15 minutes. Drain the pot and lid.

Place parchment paper in the bottom of the pot. Pour in the wine and lime juice. Add the flounder. Season with the white pepper and celery seeds; top with the shallots.

Cover the pot, and place in a cold oven. Set oven to 375°F (190°C) and cook until the fish flakes easily when probed with the tip of a knife, 30 minutes.

While the flounder is cooking, combine the cucumber, oranges, chives, oil, vinegar, red pepper, and cilantro in a small bowl. Chill for 15 to 20 minutes. Serve with the flounder.

Per serving: 178 calories, 2.6 g fat, 97 mg sodium, 0.5 g dietary fiber.

Quick tip: Shallots are closely related to onions. Use the two interchangeably, if you wish.

Mahi-Mahi with Persimmons

Get psyched for a mouth-watering experience. This exotic dish calls for mahi-mahi – a firm, flavorful, somewhat fatty fish that also goes by the name dorado – and persimmons, the national fruit of Japan.

Makes 4 servings

- 1 pound mahi-mahi fillets
- ½ cup white grape juice
- ¼ teaspoon allspice
- ¼ cup fresh cilantro leaves
- 1 small onion, sliced
- 1 persimmon, sliced

Soak a medium-size clay pot and lid in water for 10 to 15 minutes. Drain the pot and lid. Line the pot with parchment paper. Arrange the mahi-mahi in the pot. Pour in the grape juice and season with the allspice. Top with the cilantro, onions, and persimmons.

Cover the pot, and place in a cold oven. Set oven to 400°F (204°C), and cook until the mahi-mahi is done throughout and flakes easily when probed with a fork, 40 to 45 minutes.

Per serving: 189 calories, 1.1 g fat, 102 mg sodium, 0.4 g dietary fiber.

Quick tip: The Japanese persimmon (aka Hachiya) is the most widely available variety in the U.S. Use it when completely ripe and quite soft; its flavor will be tangy–sweet. When underripe, the Hachiya is extremely astringent.

Lemon–Orange Roughy

This lively fish entrée is unusually tart and tangy, thanks to lemon slices and orange juice. Sesame seeds provide a rich mellowness. Be sure to use toasted seeds; they have the richest flavor.

Makes 4 servings

- 6 sprigs fresh lemon thyme
- 1 pound orange roughy fillets
- ½ cup orange juice
- ¼ teaspoon lemon pepper
- 1 shallot, chopped
- 1 lemon, sliced
- 2 teaspoons toasted sesame seeds, for garnish

Soak a medium-size clay pot and lid in water for 10 to 15 minutes. Drain the pot and lid. Arrange the lemon thyme in the bottom of the pot. Arrange the orange roughy over the sprigs. Pour the orange juice over the fillets. Season with the lemon pepper and shallots. Top with the lemon slices.

Cover the pot, and place in a cold oven. Set oven to 400°F (204°C), and cook until the orange roughy is done throughout and flakes easily when probed with a fork, 35 to 45 minutes.

Garnish with the sesame seeds and serve immediately.

Per serving: 106 calories, 1 g fat, 94 mg sodium, 1.3 g dietary fiber.

Quick tip: Most orange roughy, which hails from New Zealand, arrives at the market frozen. If you purchase thawed fillets, do not refreeze them. The process of thawing, refreezing, and thawing will lower the quality.

Perch with Duck Sauce and Pineapple

Here's an unforgettably tasty combination of sweet (pineapple and apple juice) and savory (scallions and tomatillos) that gives perch a fresh take.

Makes 4 servings

   ½ cup apple juice

   4 teaspoons duck sauce

   1 pound perch fillets

   2 scallions, sliced in strips

   2 tomatillos, thinly sliced

   2 pineapple rings

   Chinese chili sauce (optional)

Soak a medium-size clay pot and lid in water for 10 to 15 minutes. Drain the pot and lid. Line the pot with parchment paper. Pour in the apple juice. Spread the duck sauce over the perch. Arrange in the pot. Top with the scallions, tomatillos, and pineapple rings.

Cover the pot, and place in a cold oven. Set oven to 400°F (204°C), and cook until the perch is done throughout and flakes easily when pierced with a fork, 40 to 45 minutes. Serve immediately with a small dab of the Chinese chili sauce, if desired.

Per serving: 142 calories, 1.4 g fat, 93 mg sodium, 0.8 g dietary fiber.

Quick tip: Use Chinese chili sauce sparingly; it's hot stuff!

Rainbow Trout with Orange

Farm-raised trout and fresh oranges play a delightful duet in this flavorful entrée. You'll win accolades, guaranteed.

Makes 4 servings

- 1 pound rainbow trout fillets
- ½ cup clam juice
- ¼ teaspoon lemon pepper
- 6 sprigs lemon thyme
- 2 oranges, thinly sliced

Soak a medium-size clay pot and lid in water for 10 to 15 minutes. Drain the pot and lid. Line pot with parchment paper. Arrange the trout in the pot. Pour in the clam juice. Season with the lemon pepper. Top with the thyme sprigs and orange slices from 1 orange.

Cover the pot, and place in a cold oven. Set oven to 400°F (204°C), and cook until the trout is done and flakes easily when probed with a fork, about 45 minutes. Discard the thyme sprigs. Serve with the fresh orange slices.

Per serving: 151 calories, 3.9 g fat, 121 mg sodium, 0.8 g dietary fiber.

Quick tip: If you can't find lemon thyme in your market, use the standard variety.

Scallops Edam

Haul in some well-earned compliments with this extra-easy dish. The tender sea scallops play well with creamy Edam cheese and its subtle smoky flavors.

Makes 4 servings

½ cup clam juice

½ cup dry vermouth

6 cloves garlic, crushed

1 teaspoon olive oil

⅛ teaspoon white pepper

¼ teaspoon dried tarragon leaves

1 pound sea scallops

½ cup shredded Edam cheese

Parsley sprigs, for garnish

Soak a medium-size clay pot and lid in water for 10 to 15 minutes. Meanwhile, combine the clam juice, vermouth, garlic, oil, pepper, and tarragon in a small bowl. Drain the clay pot and lid. Line the pot with parchment paper. Arrange the scallops in the pot and pour in the clam juice mixture.

Cover the pot, and place in a cold oven. Set oven to 400°F (204°C), and cook until done and opaque, 35 to 45 minutes. Transfer to a serving dish. Top with the Edam and garnish with the parsley.

Per serving: 199 calories, 6.4 g fat, 449 mg sodium, 0.1 g dietary fiber.

Quick tip: Halve or quarter large scallops so all pieces are a uniform size for even cooking.

Simply Monkfish

Poor man's lobster, as monkfish is often called, just got better in this extra-easy-to-prepare dish. It's succulent. It's delicious, thanks to Asian fish sauce, a dab of butter, and fresh chives. And it's fit for a feast — on any week night or weekend.

Makes 4 servings

- ¼ cup clam juice
- ¼ cup dry white wine
- ½ teaspoon Asian fish sauce
- 2 bay leaves
- 1 pound monkfish fillets, membranes removed
- 2 teaspoons whipped butter
- ½ cup minced fresh chives

Soak a medium-size clay pot and lid in water for 10 to 15 minutes. Meanwhile, combine the clam juice, wine, fish sauce, and bay leaves in a small bowl. Drain the clay pot and lid. Line the pot with parchment paper. Arrange the monkfish in the pot. Pour in the clam juice mixture. Dot the monkfish with the butter. Top with the chives.

Cover the pot, and place in a cold oven. Set oven to 400°F (204°C), and cook until the fish is cooked throughout and flakes easily when probed with a fork, about 45 minutes.

Per serving: 104 calories, 2.4 g fat, 288 mg sodium, 0.2 g dietary fiber.

Quick tip: Removing monkfish's grayish membrane is fairly easy. Simply lift it with your fingers and, using scissors, snip any places where it clings to the white flesh.

Szechuan Salmon

Here, salmon gets its smart, spicy flavor from just a smidgen of Szechuan sauce. Look for the sauce in the Asian section of almost any supermarket.

Makes 4 servings

  3 shallots, chopped

  ½ green bell pepper, chopped

  1 scallion, white part only, chopped

  1 pound salmon fillet

  ½ cup Chardonnay

  1 tablespoon Szechuan sauce

Soak a medium-size clay pot and lid in water for 10 to 15 minutes. Meanwhile, combine the shallots, peppers, and scallions in a small bowl. Drain the pot and lid. Line the pot with parchment paper. Arrange the salmon in the pot. Pour in the Chardonnay. Brush the Szechuan sauce over the salmon. Top with the shallot mixture.

Cover the pot, and place in a cold oven. Set oven to 400°F (204°C), and cook until the salmon is done throughout and flakes easily when probed with a fork, 40 to 50 minutes.

Per serving: 203 calories, 7.3 g fat, 173 mg sodium, 0.3 g dietary fiber.

Quick tip: Select shallots as you would onions: Choose only those that are firm and dry. Pass up any that are sprouted, soft, or blemished.

Cinnamon–Walnut Bread

Here's a raisin-studded breakfast bread that's packed with the superb nutty taste of wheat and walnuts. For peak flavor, toast it lightly right before serving.

Makes 2 loaves

3–4 cups bread flour

2 cups whole wheat flour

1½ teaspoons salt

¼ cup nonfat dry milk powder

4 teaspoons active dry yeast

1¾ cups warm water (120 to 130°F, 49 to 55°C)

¼ cup honey

2 teaspoons canola oil

1 egg, beaten

All-purpose flour, for work surfaces

Butter-flavored cooking spray

⅔ cup sugar

1 tablespoon cinnamon

1 cup raisins, plumped

¼ cup finely chopped walnuts

Soak a medium-size clay pot and lid in water for 10 to 15 minutes.

While the pot is soaking, combine 3 cups of the bread flour, the whole wheat flour, salt, powdered milk, and yeast in a large bowl, whisking to mix thoroughly.

Combine the water, honey, oil, and egg in a small bowl, whisking to blend. Pour into the flour mixture, beating to mix thoroughly. Gradually add enough of the remaining 1 cup of bread flour to form a soft dough. Sprinkle a small amount of the all-purpose flour over a work surface. Turn out the dough and knead until smooth and elastic, about 10 minutes. (Or knead in a food processor or electric mixer with dough hooks, following the manufacturer's directions.) Form into a smooth ball.

Mist a large bowl with the spray. Add the dough, turning to coat all sides with the spray. Cover the bowl with plastic wrap and a towel. Let rise for 1 hour in a warm place.

Divide the dough in half. Stretch each half to 12 x 15 inches. Mist with the spray. Sprinkle the sugar, cinnamon, raisins, and walnuts over the dough. Roll up in jelly-roll fashion, and tuck the ends under.

Drain the pot (the lid should remain in water) and line it with parchment paper. Coat with the spray. Place the rolls of dough side by side in the pot. Mist with the spray. Cover the pot with plastic wrap. Float the pot in warm water until the dough has doubled in bulk, 45 to 60 minutes, taking care not to get water in the pot. Discard the plastic wrap.

Drain the lid and wipe the inside dry. Cover the pot, and place in a cold oven. Set oven to 400°F (204°C), and bake until done, about 1¼ hours.

Per serving: 248 calories, 2.8 g fat, 232 mg sodium, 3.4 g dietary fiber.

Quick tips: To plump the raisins, soak them in warm water for 20 to 30 minutes. Drain thoroughly before using. While the dough is rising for the second time, check the water temperature fairly often. If it begins to cool, add more warm water. Don't let the dough over-rise or it will partially collapse as it bakes.

Dark Wheat Bread

This hearty wheat bread gets its spunky flavor and dark color from molasses and cocoa.

Makes 2 loaves

2–2½ cups bread flour

3 cups whole wheat flour

¼ cup nonfat dry milk powder

2 teaspoons cocoa

1 teaspoon salt

2 packages quick-rising yeast

2 cups warm water (120 to 130°F, 49 to 55°C)

3 tablespoons molasses

2 tablespoons canola oil

All-purpose flour, for work surface

Butter-flavored cooking spray

Soak a medium-size clay pot and lid in water for 10 to 15 minutes.

While the pot is soaking, combine 1½ cups of the bread flour, the whole wheat flour, powdered milk, cocoa, salt, and yeast in a large bowl, whisking to mix thoroughly.

Combine the water, molasses, and oil in a small bowl, whisking to blend. Pour into the flour mixture, beating to mix thoroughly. Gradually add enough of the remaining 1 cup of bread flour to form a soft dough.

Sprinkle a small amount of the all-purpose flour over a work surface. Turn out the dough and knead until smooth and elastic, about 10 minutes. (Or knead in a food processor or electric mixer with dough hooks, following the manufacturer's directions.) Form into a smooth ball.

Mist a large bowl with the spray. Add the dough, turning to coat all sides with the spray. Cover the bowl with plastic wrap and a towel. Let rise for 1 hour in a warm place.

Divide the dough in half. Stretch each half to 12 × 15 inches. Roll up jelly-roll fashion and tuck the ends under.

Drain the clay pot (the lid should remain in water) and line it with parchment paper. Coat with the spray. Place the rolls of dough side-by-side in the pot. Mist with the spray. Cover the pot with plastic wrap. Float the pot in warm water until the dough has doubled in bulk, 45 to 60 minutes, taking care not to get water in the pot. Discard the plastic wrap.

Drain the lid and wipe the inside dry. Cover the pot, and place in a cold oven. Set oven to 400°F (204°C), and bake until done, about 1¼ hours.

Per serving: 162 calories, 1.6 g fat, 156 mg sodium, 3.4 g dietary fiber.

Quick tips: While the dough is rising for the second time, check the water temperature fairly often. If it begins to cool, add more warm water. Don't let the dough over-rise or it will partially collapse as it bakes.

Cheddar Cheese Bread

Searching for a truly cheesy bread? Not one with a cotton-like texture and artificial coloring, but one bursting with real cheese flavor? It's here. And it's outstanding. Try it thickly sliced and toasted.

Makes 2 loaves

  5–6 cups bread flour

  2 packages quick-rising yeast

  2 tablespoons sugar

  1½ teaspoon salt

  2 teaspoons paprika

  2 tablespoons canola oil

  2 cups warm water (120 to 130°F, 49 to 55°C)

  All-purpose flour, for work surface

  2 cups shredded extra-sharp cheddar cheese

  Butter-flavored cooking spray

Soak a medium-size clay pot and lid in water for 10 to 15 minutes. While the pot is soaking, combine 5 cups of the bread flour with the yeast, sugar, salt, and paprika in a large bowl, whisking to mix thoroughly.

Combine the water and oil in a small bowl, whisking to blend. Pour into the flour mixture, beating to mix thoroughly. Gradually add enough of the remaining 1 cup of bread flour to form a soft dough.

Sprinkle a small amount of the all-purpose flour over a work surface. Turn out the dough and knead until smooth and elastic, about 10 minutes, incorporating the cheese. (Or knead in a food processor or electric mixer with dough hooks, following the manufacturer's directions.) Form into a smooth ball.

Mist a large bowl with the spray. Add the dough, turning to coat all sides with the spray. Cover the bowl with plastic wrap and a towel. Let rise for 45 minutes in a warm place.

Divide the dough in half. Stretch each half to 12 x 15 inches. Roll up jelly-roll fashion and tuck the ends under.

Drain the clay pot (the lid should remain in water) and line it with parchment paper. Coat with the spray. Place the rolls of dough side by side in the pot. Mist with the spray. Cover the pot with plastic wrap. Float the pot in warm water until the dough has doubled in bulk, 45 to 60 minutes, taking care not to get water in the pot. Discard the plastic wrap.

Drain the lid and wipe the inside dry. Cover the pot, and place in a cold oven. Set oven to 400°F (204°C), and bake until done, about 1 hour.

Per serving: 268 calories, 7.3 g fat, 308 mg sodium, 1.4 g dietary fiber.

Quick tips: For intense cheese flavor, be sure to use extra-sharp cheddar. While the dough is rising for the second time, check the water temperature fairly often. If it begins to cool, add more warm water. Don't let the dough over-rise or it will partially collapse as it bakes.

Sesame Rolls

These rolls are just the right size — not too big, not too small — for burger buns. Or they can be used for other rustic, satisfying sandwiches. Instant yeast keeps rising times short, so you can make the rolls in the morning to enjoy at lunchtime.

Makes 4 large

1¾–2½ cups bread flour

1 cup whole wheat flour

¼ cup nonfat dry milk powder

1 tablespoon sugar

1 teaspoon salt

2 packages quick-rising yeast

1 cup warm water (120 to 130°F, 49 to 55°C)

2 tablespoons canola oil

All-purpose flour, for work surface

Butter-flavored cooking spray

1 egg white

1 tablespoon cool water

½ teaspoon sesame seeds

Soak a medium-size clay pot and lid in water for 10 to 15 minutes.

While the pot is soaking, combine 1¾ cups of bread flour, the whole wheat flour, milk, salt, sugar, and yeast in a large bowl, whisking to mix thoroughly.

Combine the warm water and oil in a small bowl, whisking to blend. Pour into the flour mixture, beating to mix thoroughly. Gradually add enough of the remaining ¾ cup of bread flour to form a soft dough.

Sprinkle a small amount of the all-purpose flour over a work surface. Turn out the dough and knead until smooth and elastic, about 10 minutes. (Or knead in a food processor or electric mixer with dough hooks, following the manufacturer's directions.) Form into a smooth ball.

Mist a large bowl with the spray. Add the dough, turning to coat all sides with the spray. Cover the bowl with plastic wrap and a towel. Let rise for 1 hour. Divide the dough into 4 large or 6 small balls.

Drain the clay pot (the lid should remain in water) and line it with parchment paper. Coat with the spray. Place the dough balls in the pot. Combine the egg white and cool water. Whisk to combine. Brush over the dough. Sprinkle with the seeds. Mist with the spray. Cover the pot with plastic wrap. Float the pot in warm water until the dough has doubled in bulk, 20 to 30 minutes, taking care not to get water in the pot. Discard the plastic wrap.

Drain the lid and wipe the inside dry. Cover the pot, and place in a cold oven. Set oven to 425°F (218°C), and bake until done, 30 to 40 minutes.

Per serving: 341 calories, 6 g fat, 416 mg sodium, 4.2 g dietary fiber.

Quick tips: For a change of pace, top the rolls with poppy seeds. To make smaller rolls, divide the dough into 8 balls. While the dough is rising for the second time, check the water temperature fairly often. If it begins to cool, add more warm water. Don't let the dough over-rise or it will partially collapse as it bakes.

Just Desserts

Apple–Plum Crisp

Most fruit crisps have soft tops. Not this one. Fresh from the oven, the top is crisp and crunchy, thanks to an egg white and almond slices. Macintosh apples form the sweet, fruity base. Prefer apples slices that are a little less sweet and hold their shape when cooked? Then try the Golden Delicious or Granny Smith variety.

Makes 6 servings

> 6 Macintosh apples, peeled and sliced
>
> 3 plums, peeled and sliced
>
> Juice of ½ lemon
>
> 1 cup quick oats
>
> 1 cup packed dark brown sugar
>
> 1 teaspoon ground cinnamon
>
> ¼ teaspoon ground ginger
>
> ¼ cup almond slices
>
> 2 tablespoons canola oil
>
> 1 egg white, lightly beaten

Soak a medium-size clay pot and lid in water for 10 to 15 minutes. Drain the pot and lid. Line the bottom of the pot with parchment paper. Arrange the apples and plums in the pot. Sprinkle the lemon juice over the fruit.

Cover the pot, and place in a cold oven. Set oven to 375°F (190°C), and cook for 40 minutes.

While the fruit is cooking, combine the oats, sugar, cinnamon, ginger, almonds, oil and egg white, beating with a fork until well mixed. The mixture will be crumbly. Sprinkle over the fruit. Bake, uncovered, until the topping is puffed and golden brown, about 20 minutes. Serve with low-fat vanilla yogurt or nonfat whipped topping.

Per serving: 361 calories, 8.9 g fat, 25 mg sodium, 5.2 g dietary fiber.

Quick tips: For a more pronounced flavor, toast the almonds before adding them to the topping.

Regular oats can be substituted for the quick oats.

Ginger-Poached Pears

There's nothing shy about these pears. During cooking, they soak up the sensational flavors of rum, cinnamon and crystallized ginger and become subtly sweet yet slightly spicy. Serve them warm or at room temperature and top each half with a dollop of your favorite lemon sherbet.

Makes 4 servings

  4 Bosc pears, peeled, cored, and halved

  3 cups unsweetened apple juice

  ¼ cup light rum

  1 teaspoon chopped crystallized ginger

  1 cinnamon stick

  1 lemon, sliced

Soak a medium-size clay pot and lid in water for 10 to 15 minutes. Drain the pot and lid. Arrange the pears in the pot. Combine the juice, rum, and ginger, and pour the mixture over the pears. Add the cinnamon. Arrange the lemon slices over the pears.

Cover the pot, and place in a cold oven. Set oven to 375°F (190°C), and cook the pears for 1 hour. Remove the pot from the oven and place it on a towel or pot holders to cool. Serve the pears and poaching liquid warm or at room temperature, discarding the cinnamon stick and lemon slices.

Per serving: 315 calories, 1.3 g fat, 8 mg sodium, 5.6 g dietary fiber.

Quick tip: For best results, use slightly underripe pears.

Mixed Fruit Compote

Most cooks have a favorite dried fruit compote recipe. Here's mine. It's a tasty combination that's ideal for breakfast, brunch, or dessert. Dry white wine, orange peel, cinnamon, and cloves tone down the dried fruit's sweetness.

Makes 4 servings

> 3 cups unsweetened apple juice
>
> 1 package (8 ounces) mixed dried fruit
>
> ¾ cup raisins
>
> 1 orange, sectioned and chopped
>
> 3 strips (about 2 x 3 inches each) orange peel
>
> ½ cup dry, fruity white wine, such as Riesling
>
> 1 stick cinnamon
>
> 2 whole cloves

Soak a medium-size clay pot and lid in water for 10 to 15 minutes. Drain the lid and pot. Pour the juice into the pot. Stir in the dried fruit, raisins, orange, orange peel, wine, cinnamon, and cloves.

Cover the pot, and place in a cold oven. Set oven to 375°F (190°C), and cook the fruit for 1 hour. Remove the pot from the oven and place it on a towel or pot holders to cool. Serve the fruit and poaching liquid warm or at room temperature, discarding the cinnamon stick and orange peel.

Per serving: 360 calories, 0.7 g fat, 15 mg sodium, 6.8 g dietary fiber.

Quick tip: When cutting orange peel, take care not to cut deeply into the white part (pith); it tastes bitter.

Mocha Bread Pudding

Hooked on chocolaty-coffee flavors? Then you'll adore this pudding. It's satisfyingly rich-tasting but low in fat. Like most bread puddings, this one is best when made with a hearty country-style bread.

Makes 6 servings

  4 tablespoons cocoa

  1 cup hot coffee

  1 egg

  ¼ cup fat-free egg substitute

  2 cups low-fat (1%) milk

  1 cup skim milk

  ½ cup sugar

  1 teaspoon vanilla

  6 slices dry firm white bread, cubed

  ½ teaspoon ground cinnamon

  Nonfat whipped topping (optional)

Whisk the cocoa into the coffee in a small bowl or a 2-cup measure. Let cool. Soak a medium-size clay pot and lid in water for 10 to 15 minutes.

While the coffee is cooling and the pot soaking, lightly beat the egg and egg substitute in a medium-size bowl. Stir in the coffee mixture, low-fat milk, skim milk, sugar, and vanilla.

Drain the pot and lid. Line the pot with parchment paper. Arrange the bread in the pot. Pour in the milk mixture. Using the back of a spoon, press the bread down to moisten all pieces. Sprinkle the cinnamon over the bread.

Cover the pot, and place in a cold oven. Set oven to 375°F (190°C), and cook until a knife inserted in the center comes out clean, 45 to 60 minutes. Let cool to room temperature. Serve with whipped topping.

Per serving: 192 calories, 2 g fat, 215 mg sodium, 0.7 g dietary fiber.

Quick tip: Stored in a covered container in the refrigerator, the pudding will keep for 2 to 3 days.

Pear–Strawberry Crisp

This sweet treat takes advantage of three luscious fruits: apples, pears, and strawberries. But you could use all apples or all pears plus the berries of your choice. Optional crystallized ginger adds spicy bite for diners who like a little zing in their desserts.

Makes 6 servings

- 3 Gala apples, peeled and sliced
- 3 Bosc pears, peeled and sliced
- 3 cups fresh or frozen and thawed unsweetened whole strawberries
- 1 cup white grape juice
- 2 tablespoons quick tapioca
- ½ cup unbleached flour
- ½ cup whole wheat flour
- 1 cup sugar
- 1 tablespoon canola oil
- 1 egg white, slightly beaten
- 1 teaspoon baking powder
- 2 teaspoons minced crystallized ginger (optional)

Soak a medium-size clay pot and lid in water for 10 to 15 minutes. Drain the pot and lid. Line the bottom of the pot with parchment paper. Combine the apples, pears, strawberries, grape juice, and tapioca in a large bowl, tossing gently to mix thoroughly. Pour into the pot.

Cover the pot, and place in a cold oven. Set oven to 375°F (190°C), and cook for 40 minutes.

While the fruit is baking, combine the unbleached flour, whole wheat flour, sugar, oil, egg white, baking powder, and crystallized ginger, if using. After the 40 minutes are up, sprinkle over the fruit. Bake, uncovered, until the topping is puffed and golden brown, about 25 to 30 minutes. Serve with low-fat vanilla yogurt or nonfat whipped topping.

Per serving: 371 calories, 3.2 g fat, 79 mg sodium, 6 g dietary fiber.

Quick tip: Crystallized ginger is hard and sticky. To mince it, use a heavy sharp chef's knife or sharp kitchen scissors.

Pineapple–Rice Pudding

Exceptionally quick to assemble, this light goodie makes for a grand finale. Serve it after lunch or dinner or as a mid-afternoon snack. For a creamier pudding, replace the fat-free milk with the 1% variety.

Makes 4 servings

3 cups fat-free milk

¼ cup basmati brown rice or medium-grain brown rice

1 egg, lightly beaten

½ cup sugar

½ teaspoon vanilla extract

1 cup drained pineapple chunks

Soak a medium-size clay pot and lid in water for 10 to 15 minutes. Combine the milk, rice, egg, and sugar.

Drain the pot and lid. Pour the milk–rice mixture into the pot. Cover the pot, and place in a cold oven. Set oven to 375°F (190°C), and cook until the pudding is thick and the rice tender, 45 to 60 minutes. Stir in the vanilla and pineapple. Serve warm or chilled.

Per serving: 247 calories, 1.8 g fat, 111 mg sodium, 0.5 g dietary fiber.

Quick tip: Stored in a covered container in the refrigerator, the pudding will keep for 2 to 3 days.

Warm Fresh Fruit Delight

This delicate, refreshing dessert focuses on five favorite fruits: apples, pears, oranges, grapes, and nectarines. If juicy nectarines are elusive, try frozen peaches instead. The seasoning in this dish is subtle; if you want something spicier, add lemon juice and a dash of mace.

Makes 6 servings

- 2 cups white grapes
- 2 nectarines, peeled and sliced
- 2 Anjou pears, peeled and cubed
- 2 Golden Delicious apples, peeled and cubed
- 2 oranges, peeled and sectioned
- 1 stick cinnamon
- ¼ teaspoon ground nutmeg
- 1 cup orange juice
- 2 cups low-fat vanilla yogurt, frozen low-fat vanilla yogurt, or orange sherbet

Soak a medium-size clay pot and lid in water for 10 to 15 minutes. Drain the pot and lid.

Combine the grapes, nectarines, pears, apples, oranges, cinnamon, nutmeg, and orange juice in the pot. Toss gently to mix. Cover the pot, and place in a cold oven. Set oven to 375°F (190°C), and cook for 30 minutes.

Discard the cinnamon; stir to mix. Let cool, covered, for 5 minutes. Serve immediately topped with the yogurt, frozen yogurt, or sherbet.

Per serving: 209 calories, 1.8 g fat, 54 mg sodium, 4.6 g dietary fiber.

Quick tip: Serve within 30 minutes of cooking; otherwise, the fruit will begin to darken.

Glossary

Allspice: Though this spice tastes like a combination of cinnamon, nutmeg and cloves, it's really just one spice, a small, dark-brown berry. Allspice flavors both savory and sweet dishes, and you can buy it whole or ground.

Bamboo shoots: These somewhat crisp, ivory-colored shoots come from an edible Asian bamboo plant. They're available fresh in Asian specialty groceries and canned in the ethnic aisles of most supermarkets.

Basmati rice: Grown primarily in the Himalayan foothills of northern India and Pakistan, basmati is a white or brown long-grain rice that has been aged to reduce its moisture content. When cooked, basmati has a perfumy aroma and nutty flavor; the grains remain dry and separate. Look for this exotic rice in Middle Eastern groceries, health food stores, and large supermarkets.

Bay leaf: May also be called *bay laurel* or *laurel leaf.* This herb, which is rarely available fresh, is a standard component of a *bouquet garni* and of pickling spice; it provides subtle flavor to soups, stews, and other saucy dishes. Always discard it at the end of cooking.

Bell peppers: *See* **Peppers.**

Black-eyed pea: Also called a *cowpea,* this legume is small and beige with an oval black "eye" at the center of its curve. Its texture is mealy; its flavor, earthy. Look for black-eyed peas fresh, frozen, canned, or dried.

Blanch: To partially cook fruits or vegetables by steaming or dipping them for 30 seconds to 2 minutes into boiling water, then plunging them into cold water to stop the cooking process. Blanching is often used to set flavor and color or to loosen skins.

Bok choy: This relative of Chinese cabbage has crunchy, juicy white stalks and tender dark green leaves. Sometimes labeled *pak choy, pak choi, Chinese chard cabbage,* or *Chinese white cabbage,* bok choy is sweet, cabbagelike and mild. Choose bok choy with firm stalks and crisp leaves; store it in a plastic bag in the refrigerator for up to 4 days. Bok choy is a versatile player in salads, stir-fries, and Chinese dishes.

Butternut squash: A variety of hard-shelled winter squash that has a beige exterior and a deep orange-colored flesh. Though generally available year round, butternut's peak season starts in early fall and ends in late winter. Purchase butternuts that are heavy for their size and blemish free. Since they don't need refrigeration, you can stash them in a cool, dry, dark spot for a month or more.

Cajun seasoning: May also be labeled *Cajun spice seasoning.* This is a sassy blend of garlic, onion, chilies, black pepper, mustard, and celery. Each brand of this seasoning has its own exclusive combination, so all taste a little different. Try several to find the one you like best.

Caper: The flower bud of a Mediterranean shrub, the caper has a prized sour and slightly bitter flavor. Its size ranges from tiny (a French nonpareil variety) to large (an Italian variety that's as big as the end of your little finger). Once picked, the bud is sun-dried, then packed in salt or a vinegar brine. To remove some of the saltiness, rinse capers in cold water before using them. The flower buds of nasturtium, buttercup, marigold, and broom are sometimes used as inexpensive substitutes for capers.

Celery seed: This tiny pungent seed comes from lovage, a cousin to celery. Its flavor is fairly intense, so use the spice, which is available whole or ground, sparingly.

Chili powder: A hot, spicy mixture of chili peppers, oregano, cumin, salt, garlic, coriander, and cloves. For an intense blend, get one without salt. Chili powder is a mainstay in chilies and other Mexican and Tex-Mex style dishes.

Chinese chili sauce: A spicy condiment of chili peppers, garlic, and vinegar. Look for it in jars in large supermarkets or Asian specialty groceries.

Cilantro: Also called *Chinese parsley* and *fresh coriander,* cilantro is an herb with small, fragile leaves and a lively, almost musty taste. It's a signature flavor for Caribbean, Latin American, and some Asian cuisines. Choose bunches of leaves with bright, lively color and no signs of wilting. Store cilantro, unwashed, in a plastic bag in the refrigerator for up to a week. Wash the leaves just before using them.

Corned beef: A cured beef product, either brisket or round, with a deep red color and a slightly salty taste.

Cream-style corn: When commercially prepared, this corn product contains corn, sugar, and cornstarch. Homemade cream-style corn is nothing more than the pulp and juice squeezed from corn kernels.

Cremini mushrooms: This variety of common domestic mushroom (species *Agaricus bisporus)* has brown caps. The flavor is mild, and the cap size ranges from ½ to 3 inches. Buy only those that are firm and plump and have no bruises, spots, or sliminess. Keep them in the refrigerator in a paper bag (or, if prepacked, in their container) for up to 2 days. To clean them, wipe them with a damp towel. Never soak fresh mushrooms; they'll absorb too much water, which spoils their texture and dilutes their flavor.

Cumin: A small, amber-colored seed resembling a miniature caraway seed, cumin is a parsley relative with an aromatic, pungent–nutty flavor that dominates many Mexican and Indian dishes. You can find whole and ground cumin. If you have access to an Asian market, check out the white and black cumin seeds. The white and amber varieties can be used interchangeably, but the black ones have a more complex, peppery flavor.

Curry powder: Not a single spice, but a blend of up to 20 spices and herbs including cumin, coriander, red pepper, fenugreek, cinnamon, allspice, fennel, ginger, black pepper, mace, nutmeg, cloves, poppy seeds, sesame seeds, and turmeric. Turmeric gives the blend its yellow color. To eliminate any raw taste, toast curry powder in a small nonstick skillet before adding it to a recipe. Curry powder is the signature seasoning in all curry dishes.

Dijon mustard: Originating in France, this is a popular grayish brown mustard made with brown or black mustard seeds, white wine, and a blend of spices. It has a clean, sharp taste that complements many foods and dishes.

Dredge: To coat a food, such as pieces of chicken or meatballs, with a dry ingredients, such as cornmeal or flour. Dredging can add flavor and aid browning.

Duck sauce: A thick, sweet-sour condiment made with plums, apricots, sugar, and seasonings. Often referred to as plum sauce and served with duck and pork.

Fennel: Often mislabeled as sweet anise, fennel has a broad bulbous base, overlapping pale green stems, and feathery greenery. Its flavor is mildly anise- or licorice-like. Choose firm bulbs with crisp stems and bright, fresh-looking greenery. Store in a plastic bag in the refrigerator for up to 4 days.

Feta cheese: A white, crumbly cheese with a tangy flavor, feta is a classic Greek cheese made from sheep's, goat's, or cow's milk. It's cured and stored in a salty brine and makes a zesty addition to salads and other dishes.

Five-spice powder: True to its name, this lively spice blend contains five distinctive spices: cinnamon, cloves, fennel seeds, star anise, and Szechuan peppercorns. It's used in many Chinese dishes.

Garbanzo beans: Also called *chick peas,* garbanzo beans are round, light tan legumes with a firm texture and mild, nutlike flavor. They're used extensively in Middle East dishes such as hummus (a garlic- and lemon-flavored dip served with pita bread pockets). They're available dried and canned.

Ginger: A seasoning with a somewhat sweet aroma, a pungent flavor, and a peppery after-kick, ginger comes in three forms: fresh (a gnarled root), dried and ground (located with the jarred spices), and crystallized (found in small packets with candied fruits). Fresh ginger, which is often called gingerroot, makes a delicious contribution to curries, soups, and Asian-style stir-fries. Dried ginger, which should not be used as a substitute for the fresh version, adds indispensable flavor to gingerbread, gingersnaps, and ginger ale. The crystallized version, which has been cooked in a sugar syrup, jazzes up fruit compotes and the like. Fresh ginger can be stored, tightly wrapped in plastic wrap, in the refrigerator for up to 3 weeks or in the freezer for up to 6 months.

Herbes de Provence: A commercial blend of six dried herbs that's typically used in the cuisine of southern France: rosemary, marjoram, thyme, sage, anise seed, and savory. Use it to season chicken, pork, veal, fish, and shrimp dishes.

Hoisin sauce: This thick, sweet-spicy, reddish brown condiment is widely used in southern Chinese cooking. Its basic ingredients include soybeans, chili peppers, garlic, sugar, vinegar and spices. Hoisin sauce is available in Asian specialty groceries as well as most supermarkets. Once opened, it should be stored, tightly covered, in a glass jar in the refrigerator, where it'll keep for months.

Horseradish: Eye-wateringly hot, especially when fresh, horseradish is the root of a perennial plant that's grated for boosting the flavor of soups, sauces, and spreads. Bottled horseradish is a nippy condiment made of grated horseradish, white vinegar, and seasonings. Plan to use it quickly it loses its potency with age.

Hot-pepper sauce: Not a single sauce, but one of many Louisiana-style sauces made from hot chili peppers, vinegar, and salt. The heat and flavor of hot-pepper sauces vary from brand to brand. Some are relatively mild; others, so scorching that just a drop or two fires up an entire dish. When using a hot sauce for the first time, cautiously add it to soups, stews, marinades and other dishes.

Instant flour: A specially formulated flour that dissolves quickly without lumping in hot and cold liquids. It's used mostly for thickening sauces and gravies.

Italian herb seasoning: A pleasant herb blend of oregano, basil, and thyme, and sometimes red pepper, rosemary, and garlic powder. Use the mix to achieve characteristic Italian flavor without measuring out the individual seasonings.

Jasmati rice: An American variety of aromatic jasmine rice.

Jerk seasoning: Often called *Jamaican jerk seasoning,* this is a dry blend of chilies, thyme, cinnamon, ginger, allspice, cloves, garlic, and onions. Originating in Jamaica, the blend is usually rubbed on meats, especially pork or poultry, for grilling.

Kielbasa: This is a robust smoked Polish sausage that's usually sold precooked. Most kielbasa, also known as *kielbasy,* is made with pork, though beef is sometimes added. Nowadays, you can also get lower-fat turkey versions. For best flavor, always heat kielbasa before serving it.

Leek: A member of the lily family and a cousin of garlic and onion, the leek resembles a gigantic scallion. Its flavor and fragrance are mildly onionlike; its texture, crunchy. When buying leeks, look for crisp, brightly colored leaves and unblemished white portions. Slender leeks will be the most tender. To use leeks, cut off the rootlets and slit the leeks from end to end. Then swish them in cool running water to wash away sand or earth trapped between the layers.

Lemon pepper: A seasoning blend of black pepper and grated lemon zest. Check the label before buying this blend; it sometimes contains more salt than pepper or lemon.

Madeira wine: A fortified wine that's named after the Portuguese island Madeira. Its color runs from pale golden to rich tawny and its flavor can be anywhere from quite dry to very sweet.

Mandarin oranges: These are a category of thin-, loose-skinned oranges with easily separated segments. You can find fresh mandarin oranges under the names tangerines, tangelos, and clementines. Canned mandarin oranges are usually a different variety: small Japanese satsuma oranges, which are seedless.

Marjoram: Also called *sweet marjoram.* A member of the mint family, marjoram has long, oval leaves with a mild oreganolike flavor. To retain its delicate taste, add it to dishes toward the end of cooking.

Marsala: A fortified wine that's imported from Sicily. Its intriguing smoky flavor ranges from sweet to dry.

Mint: A delightful herb with a cool, refreshing aftertaste. It comes in fresh and dried forms as well as extracts. The two most popular mints are spearmint and peppermint. Of the two, spearmint is the mildest. Choose mint with fresh-looking, even-colored leaves. To store, place the bunch, stems down, in a small glass of water, and cover the glass and leaves with a plastic bag. Refrigerate the whole thing, changing the water every few days. Stored this way, the mint should stay fresh for up to a week.

Mustard seeds: These are the seeds of the mustard plant, peppery greens belonging to the same family as broccoli, brussels sprouts, kale, collards, and kohlrabi. The seeds themselves come in three varieties: black, brown, and yellow, yellow being the most common and most readily available. Left whole or cracked, mustard seeds boost the flavor of potato salad, pickles, relishes, and boiled shrimp.

Nutmeg: A hard, brownish seed with a warm, spicy, sweet flavor. It's sold ground and whole. Expect to get the best flavor from freshly ground whole nutmeg. Use nutmeg to perk up baked goods, custards, and vegetables such as potatoes and winter squash.

Orange roughy: A low-fat fish with firm white flesh and mild flavor. Hails from Australia and New Zealand. In the U.S., it's available frozen or thawed.

Paprika: A special variety of red sweet pepper pods that have been ground for use as a seasoning and a garnish. Paprika comes from several parts of the world: Spain, California, South America and Hungary. The Hungarian variety is considered by many to be a standout. After opening paprika, store it in the refrigerator, where it'll retain its bright color and flavor longest.

Pasta: A dough (or paste) made with flour and water and, sometimes, eggs. Generally speaking, pasta made with eggs is called *noodles* in the United States. You can make your own pasta or buy it fresh, frozen or dried. The last is the most popular, since it's inexpensive and keeps almost indefinitely. Dried pasta comes in at least 600 shapes.

Peppercorns: These are the berries of the pepper plant *(Piper nigrum)* that produces black and white pepper. Black pepper, the most popular, comes from the dried berry with its skin; white pepper, which is also dried, comes minus the skin. Of the two, white pepper is slightly milder and is a good choice in light-colored sauces where dark specks of black pepper would stand out.

Peppers: Crunchy, colorful, flavorful, sweet, hot, versatile, high in vitamin C. Such attributes make peppers a favored vegetable in many cuisines: Mexican, Chinese, Thai, Hungarian, to name a few. Though there are scads of pepper varieties, all can be divided into two basic categories: sweet and hot. Here's a brief rundown of several popular and readily available peppers:

> **Bell:** A sweet, bell-shaped pepper that comes in green, red, yellow, orange, brown or purple. They're suitable for stuffing, slicing and dicing. Use them to punch up color, flavor and crunch in just about any soup, stew, casserole, stir-fry or sandwich.

> **Cayenne:** A long, thin, sharply pointed, hot pepper that's either straight or curled. Generally, cayennes are sold when fully ripe and red in color.

Chipotle chili: This hot pepper is actually a smoked, dried jalapeño. Its skin is dark brown and wrinkled. Look for it plain, dried, pickled, and canned in adobo sauce.

Jalapeño: A tapered, 2-inch-long, very hot pepper that's usually sold at the green but mature stage. These peppers are used to season sausages, cheeses, and even jellies.

Pimento (pimiento): A large, heart-shaped, mild pepper that's usually sold in jars. Thick and meaty, these peppers are ideal for roasting, if you can find them fresh.

Poblano: A very dark green, moderately hot pepper that resembles a small bell pepper with a tapered blossom end.

Pickling spice: This is a pungent dried spice and herb blend used for making pickles, relishes, and other dishes. The mix varies according to manufacturer, but most include these basics: whole and broken allspice, bay leaves, cardamom, cinnamon, cloves, coriander, ginger, mace, mustard seeds, and peppercorns. It's sold in small sealed bags, boxes, and jars.

Pork tenderloin: This is an extremely lean pork loin roast cut from the hog's back. When cooked, the meat is tender and white with clear juices. Tasty ways with this cut include roasting, stir-frying, sautéing, and stewing.

Prosciutto: Usually sold in transparently thin slices, prosciutto, which in Italian means "ham," is a seasoned, salt-cured, and air-dried meat. Connoisseurs often recommend eating it as is. If you do cook it, add it to hot foods at the last minute; prolonged cooking will toughen it.

Provolone cheese: A firm Italian cheese with a mild, smoky flavor and firm texture. Made from cow's milk, Provolone makes an excellent cooking cheese and, when aged, grates nicely for use as a topping.

Recaito sauce: Similar to sofrito, a seasoning sauce popular in Hispanic cooking, recaito has a lively green color – thanks to cilantro and green peppers.

Rice noodles and sticks: Sold loosely coiled in plastic or cellophane bags, the dry rice-flour noodles are extremely thin and long and resemble white hair or threads. Soak them in water, and they explode into an airy tangle of strands ready for soups or stir-fries. Rice sticks are ⅓-inch-wide rice noodles. Look for both of these high-starch, low-protein products in Asian groceries and large supermarkets.

Ricotta cheese: *Ricotta* means "recooked" in Italian. Made from a combination of cooked whey (a by-product of cheesemaking and, hence, the term *recooked)* and milk, ricotta is a white, moist, fresh cheese. It often serves as the filling in savory dishes, such as lasagna and stuffed shells, and in desserts such as cheesecake.

Romano cheese: A nippy Italian cheese with a light yellow color and hard texture similar to that of Parmesan cheese. May be from sheep's, goat's, or cow's milk. Romano is generally grated and often is added to Italian-style dishes. For maximum flavor, use it freshly grated.

Rosemary: The green leaves of this aromatic Mediterranean herb resemble pine needles, and many cooks describe its taste as somewhat piny. Chop fresh leaves before using them and crush the dried form in a mortar and pestle. Rosemary is fairly assertive, especially when fresh, so apply it with restraint in vinaigrettes, sauces, lamb and chicken dishes.

Sage: Sporting grayish-green leaves, which have a soft velvetlike surface, sage is an herb native to the Mediterranean. Its flavor stands out, pleasantly so, in traditional sausage mixes as well as in poultry stuffings. When buying fresh sage, look for bunches of leaves with no blemishes or wilting. Keep sage, unwashed, in a plastic bag in the refrigerator for up to 4 days. Dried sage comes whole, rubbed (crumbled), and ground. Feel free to interchange rubbed and ground varieties in recipes. Because dried sage loses its spunk within 3 months, get it in small quantities.

Shallots: Though related to onions, shallots look more like giant, brown garlic bulbs than onions. A shallot bulb is composed of multiple cloves, each covered with a thin, dry, papery skin. When selecting shallots, choose those that are plump and firm with no signs of wilting or sprouting. Keep them in a cool, well-ventilated spot for up to a month. Mild in flavor, shallots can be used in the same manner as onions.

Smoke flavoring: Available in liquid form, smoke flavoring is nothing more than smoke concentrate in a water base.

Sofrito: Many Spanish and Caribbean recipes call for this thick, flavorful sauce as a seasoning. Traditionally it's made with annatto seeds, pork (or rendered pork fat), onions, sweet peppers, garlic, and herbs. Look for sofrito in jars in the international section of your supermarket, and use just a tablespoon or two to pump up any soup that needs a little special character.

Stir-fry: To cook bite-size pieces of food quickly in a small amount of oil over high heat while stirring constantly and briskly. Also refers to a dish that has been prepared by stir-frying.

Sweet potato: Two varieties of sweet potato are commonly available in most supermarkets: a dry type with light yellow flesh and a moist type with reddish orange flesh. The moist variety is the sweeter of the two and is often mislabeled as a "yam." Look for small to medium potatoes with smooth, blemish-free skin, and store them in a cool, dry, dark place for up to a week. Sweet potatoes are a superb source of vitamin A.

Swiss chard: Sometimes called *chard* or *rhubarb chard,* this member of the beet family has big dark green leaves and large, deep-red or white celery-like stalks. A cruciferous cousin, cooked chard is a powerhouse of vitamins A, C, and folate. When selecting chard, look for crisp leaves and stalks, and remember that a pound cooks down to about a single cup. Store fresh leaves in a plastic bag in the refrigerator for up to 3 days.

Szechuan sauce: A spicy Chinese condiment of miso, broad beans, rice wine vinegar, soy beans and red peppers. Available in jars in large supermarkets.

Szechuan seasoning: This widely available blend of ginger, black pepper, red pepper, garlic, and paprika captures the essence of Szechuan flavor accents.

Tamarillo: Also called a *tree tomato,* the tamarillo is related to the tomato and hails from Peru. The fruit is about the size of an egg, with an inedible shiny yellow or burgundy skin; a firm, slightly tart flesh; and edible black seeds. Select tamarillos that are firm with blemish-free, glossy skin. When ripe, they will yield to slight pressure and be fragrant. Avoid unripe tamarillos; they're often bitter. Store ripe tamarillos in a plastic bag in the refrigerator for up to 2 weeks. Enjoy cooked or raw.

Tarragon: An herb, popular in French cooking, with a distinctive, almost licoricelike taste. Tarragon's slender, pointed and dark green leaves flavor such foods as chicken, Béarnaise, and fines herbes. Use tarragon with a little caution; its assertiveness can easily overwhelm other flavors.

Teriyaki: A delightful homemade or commercially prepared Japanese sauce made of soy sauce, sake (or sherry), sugar, ginger, and garlic. *Teriyaki* also refers to any dish made with a teriyaki sauce.

Tetrazzini: This main-dish casserole traditionally contains chicken or turkey, spaghetti, mushrooms, and almonds in a rich sherry-cream sauce. Before baking, the casserole is often sprinkled with grated cheese.

Texmati: A variety of Indian basmati rice that is grown in Texas. It's readily available in white and brown versions.

Thai spice: An exotic blend of chili peppers, ginger, coriander, cumin, cinnamon, star anise, garlic, lemon peel, and dried shallots that may be labeled *Thai seasoning.* It imparts warm, robust flavor to noodles, rice, soups, and other dishes.

Tortilla: Made from corn *(masa)* or wheat flour, tortillas are thin, flat, round unleavened Mexican breads that resemble pancakes. Traditionally, they're baked, but not browned, on a griddle. Tortillas can be eaten plain or wrapped around a multitude of fillings to create tacos, burritos, enchiladas, tostadas and chimichangas. Pick up prepackaged tortillas in the refrigerator section of your supermarket and store them according to package directions.

Tomatillo: A signature ingredient in *salsa verde,* the tomatillo is a small green fruit that's covered by a thin, papery, brown husk. The fruit has flavor hints of lemon, apple, and spices and is often used in Mexican and Tex-Mex foods. Choose tomatillos with tight-fitting, dry husks and no signs of mold. Store tomatillos in a paper bag in the refrigerator for up to a month. Before using these somewhat tart fruits, remove and discard the husks and wash the fruit.

Turmeric: Probably best known for the distinctive bright yellow color it gives American-style prepared mustards, turmeric is a musty, bittersweet spice related to ginger. Use this dried powder sparingly; it's pretty intense stuff – so intense, in fact, that it will stain plastic utensils. Turmeric is an inexpensive substitute for saffron.

Whisk: To beat light liquids or eggs with a wire whisk (a utensil made of looped wires held together by a handle) until blended. A whisk may also be used to blend flour and other light dry ingredients.

Wild pecan rice: This is a delightful aromatic rice, sometimes labeled simply *pecan rice,* that hails from Louisiana. It has a wonderful nutty flavor, and the grains remain fluffy and separate after cooking.

Worcestershire sauce: A dark, pungent condiment made from soy sauce, vinegar, garlic, tamarind, onions, molasses, lime, anchovies, and other seasonings, Worcestershire sauce was first concocted in India and bottled in Worcestershire, England. Use it to flavor soups, meats, gravies, and vegetable juices.

Everyday Equivalents

Recalling most measures – for example, 8 ounces equal a cup and others we use everyday – is a snap. But those used once a decade (at least it seems that seldom) easily slip our minds. To jog your memory and help you measure up, refer to this table of U.S. to metric equivalents, rounded for easy use.

U. S. Units			Metric
Liquids			
¼ teaspoon			1 milliliter
½ teaspoon			2 milliliters
1 teaspoon	60 drops	⅙ fluid ounce	5 milliliters
1 tablespoon	3 teaspoons	½ fluid ounce	15 milliliters
2 tablespoons	⅛ cup	1 fluid ounce	30 milliliters
4 tablespoons	¼ cup	2 fluid ounces	60 milliliters
5⅓ tablespoons	⅓ cup	2⅔ fluid ounces	80 milliliters
8 tablespoons	½ cup	4 fluid ounces	113 milliliters
1 cup	16 tablespoons	8 fluid ounces	236 milliliters
2 cups	1 pint	16 fluid ounces	500 milliliters
4 cups	1 quart	32 fluid ounces	1 liter
4 quarts	1 gallon	128 fluid ounces	3¾ liters

Temperature		Weight	
32°F	0°C	1 ounce	28.35 grams
212°F	100°C	4 ounces	115 grams
350°F	177°C	8 ounces	225 grams
375°F	190°C	16 ounces (1 pound)	454 grams
400°F	204°C	32 ounces (2 pounds)	907 grams
425°F	218°C	36 ounces (2¼ pounds)	1000 grams
450°F	232°C		

Winning Ways with
Herbs and Spices

A pinch of herbs or spices can do wonders for a soup needing more jazz or a chowder in need of pizzazz. But knowing what seasoning to pair with what food can be daunting even for an accomplished cook. To help you find a good match, here are some classic, palate-pleasing combinations.

HERBS

Herb	Flavor	Meat, Poultry, Fishes, Dairy	Vegetables
Basil	Pungent licorice	Beef. chicken, lamb, salmon, turkey, tuna	Asparagus, beets, broccoli, cabbage, carrots, cucumbers, eggplant, mushrooms, potatoes, summer squash, tomatoes
Bay leaf	Menthol	Beef, chicken, lamb, most fish	Artichokes, beets, carrots, potatoes, tomatoes
Chervil	Light licorice, parsleylike	Beef, chicken, fish, lamb, shellfish, pork, turkey	Asparagus, beets, carrots, eggplant, mushrooms, peas, potatoes, squash, tomatoes
Chives	Delicate, onionlike	Most fish, cheese	Potatoes, tomatoes

Herb	Flavor	Meat, Poultry, Fishes, Dairy	Vegetables
Cilantro	Distinctive pungent smell and taste	Beef	Beans, tomatoes
Dill	Tangy, carawaylike	Chicken, fish, shellfish, eggs, cheese	Avocado, beans, cabbage, cauliflower, carrots, cucumbers, green beans, parsnips, potatoes, tomatoes
Marjoram	Oreganolike	Beef, chicken, fish, shellfish, lamb, pork, veal	Brussels sprouts, carrots, corn, eggplant, mixed greens, peas, potatoes, summer squash
Mint	Menthol	Chicken, lamb, pork	Carrots, cucumbers, green beans, mixed greens, peas, potatoes, summer squash, tomatoes
Oregano	Strong, aromatic, similar to marjoram	Beef, chicken, fish, pork, shellfish, turkey, veal, eggs	Avocado, beans, broccoli, cabbage, corn, cucumbers, eggplant, mushrooms, potatoes, summer squash, tomatoes

HERB	FLAVOR	MEAT, POULTRY, FISHES, DAIRY	VEGETABLES
Parsley	Fresh herbal	Beef, chicken, fish, lamb, shellfish, pork, turkey, veal, cheese, eggs	Avocado, beans, cabbage, cauliflower, corn, cucumbers, eggplant, green beans, mixed greens, mushrooms, potatoes, summer squash, tomatoes
Rosemary	Hints of lemon and thyme	Beef, chicken, fish, shellfish, lamb, pork, turkey, veal	Cauliflower, cucumbers, green beans, mushrooms, peas, potatoes, summer squash, tomatoes, turnips
Sage	Slightly bitter, musty mint	Beef, chicken, flounder, halibut, lamb, pork, sole, veal	Beans, beets, brussels sprouts, carrots, eggplant, peas, potatoes, tomatoes, winter squash
Savory	Minty thyme	Beef, chicken, fish, lamb, shellfish, turkey	Artichokes, asparagus, beans, beets, cabbage, carrots, green beans, lentils, mixed greens, peas, potatoes, tomatoes

Herb	Flavor	Meat, Poultry, Fishes, Dairy	Vegetables
Tarragon	Aniselike	Beef, chicken, fish, lamb, shellfish, pork, veal, turkey cheese, eggs	Asparagus, beets, carrots, cauliflower, green beans, mixed greens, mushrooms, potatoes, summer and winter squash, tomatoes
Thyme	Somewhat lemonlike	Beef, chicken, clams, fish, lamb, shellfish, pork, veal, tuna, turkey, cheese, eggs	Beets, carrots, green beans, potatoes, summer squash, tomatoes

SPICES

Spice	Flavor	Meat, Poultry, Fishes, Dairy	Vegetables
Allspice	Combined taste of cinnamon, nutmeg, cloves	Beef, chicken, fish, ham, turkey, cheese, eggs	Beets, carrots, parsnips, peas, spinach, sweet potatoes, turnips, winter squash
Capers	Pungent, briny	Fish, poultry	Spinach
Caraway	Nutty, aniselike	Beef, pork, cheese	Cabbage, cucumbers, onions, potatoes, turnips, winter squash

Spice	Flavor	Meat, Poultry, Fishes, Dairy	Vegetables
Cardamom	Gingery–lemon	Chicken, fish, cheese	Beans, carrots, pumpkin, sweet potatoes, winter squash
Cayenne	Hot, peppery	Beef, chicken, fish, shellfish, lamb, pork, turkey, cheese, eggs	Beans, cabbage, carrots, cucumbers, green beans, lima beans, potatoes, spinach, tomatoes
Celery seed	Strong celery	Beef, chicken, fish, lamb, turkey, veal, cheese, eggs	Beets, cabbage, cauliflower, cucumbers, potatoes, tomatoes
Cinnamon	Pungent, bittersweet	Beef, chicken, pork	Beets, carrots, onions, pumpkin, sweet potatoes, tomatoes, winter squash
Cloves	Strong, pungent	Beef, lamb, pork	Beets, carrots, green beans, onions, pumpkin, sweet potatoes, winter squash
Coriander	Lemon–sage	Beef, chicken, fish, cheese, eggs	Beets, cauliflower, onions, potatoes, spinach, tomatoes
Cumin	Earthy, nutty	Beef, chicken, pork, salmon, shellfish, tuna	Beans, carrots, cabbage, pumpkin, tomatoes

SPICE	FLAVOR	MEAT, POULTRY, FISHES, DAIRY	VEGETABLES
Fennel	Aniselike	Beef, chicken, lamb, pork, fish, shellfish, cheese, eggs	Beets, cabbage, cucumbers, onions, peas, summer squash, tomatoes
Ginger	Sweet, pungent, peppery	Beef, chicken, fish, shellfish, lamb, pork, cheese	Avocado, cabbage, carrots, summer and winter squash, sweet potatoes
Mace	Mild nutmeg	Beef, chicken, shellfish, veal, cheese	Broccoli, brussels sprouts, cabbage, green beans, pumpkin, spinach, winter squash
Mustard	Sharp, tangy, biting	Beef, chicken, fish, ham, shellfish, pork, cheese, eggs	Beets, brussels sprouts, cabbage, cucumbers, green beans, mixed greens
Nutmeg	Spicy, nutty	Beef, chicken, ham, pork, turkey, cheese, eggs	Beans, corn, eggplant, mushrooms, onions, potatoes, pumpkin, spinach, tomatoes, winter squash
Paprika	Piquant	Beef, chicken, turkey, veal, eggs, cheese	Cauliflower, potatoes, turnips
Turmeric	Musty	Beef, chicken, pork, turkey	Beans, pumpkin, winter squash

Emergency Substitutes

Uh-oh, you've checked the pantry and looked in the refrigerator, so there's no doubt about it: you're out of nonfat sour cream, Italian herb seasoning and chili powder. Three ingredients your favorite recipe calls for, and you planned to serve the recipe tonight. What now? Check this handy table; it'll help you find quick replacements for missing items. Just remember, the substitutes may give the recipe a somewhat different flavor or texture.

RECIPE REQUIRES	QUICK SUBSTITUTE
Bacon (1 slice crumbled)	Bacon bits (1 T)
Allspice	Cinnamon; dash of nutmeg
Bread crumbs, dry (1 cup)	Cracker crumbs (¾ cup)
Broth, beef or chicken (1 cup)	Bouillon cube (1) plus boiling water (1 cup)
Chili powder (1 T)	Hot-pepper sauce (a drop or two) plus oregano (¼ t) and cumin (¼ t)
Cinnamon (1 t)	Allspice (¼ t) or nutmeg (¼ t)
Cornstarch (1 T)	All-purpose flour (2 T)
Cumin (1 t)	Chili powder (1 t)
Egg (1 whole)	Egg substitute (¼ cup)
Flour, as thickener (2 T)	Cornstarch (1 T) or quick-cooking tapioca (2 T)

Recipe Requires	Quick Substitute
Garlic (1 clove)	Garlic powder (⅛ t)
Ginger (1 t)	Allspice (½ t), cinnamon (1 t), or nutmeg (½ t)
Italian herb seasoning (1 t)	Basil, dried (1 t), plus thyme, dried leaves (1 t)
Lemon juice (1 t)	Cider vinegar (½ t)
Lemon peel (1 t grated)	Lemon extract (½ t)
Mustard, dry (1 t)	Mustard, prepared (1 T)
Mustard, prepared (1 T)	Mustard, powdered (½ t) plus vinegar (2t)
Nonfat sour cream (1 cup)	Plain nonfat yogurt (1 cup)
Onion (1 minced)	Onions, dried, minced (1 T) or onion powder (1 t)
Pumpkin pie spice	Cinnamon, ground (1 t) plus nutmeg, ground (½ t) and powdered ginger (½ t)
Seasoned bread crumbs, dry (1 cup)	Plain dry bread crumbs (⅞ cup) plus grated Parmesan cheese (1 T) and dried parsley (1 T)
Sherry (1 T)	Sherry extract (1 T)
Teriyaki sauce (1 T)	Soy sauce (1 T) plus powdered garlic (⅛ t) and minced fresh ginger (¼ t)
Tomato sauce (1 cup)	Tomato paste (½ cup) plus water (½ cup)
Vinegar (1 t)	Lemon juice (2 t)

Key to abbreviations: T = tablespoon; t = teaspoon

Culinary Math

Quick, quick! A creamy soup recipe calls for 1 cup of broccoli florets. How many pounds of fresh broccoli should you buy? A stew requires 2 cups of beef broth. How many cans should you open? Stumped? That's understandable. After all, who among us memorizes such nitty-gritty food facts? For an approximate answer (it's impossible to be exact), look to this concise table.

A

Almonds, shelled, blanched: ½ pound = 1½ cups whole = 2 cups slivered

Apples: 1 pound = 3 medium = 2¾ to 3 cups chopped or sliced

Apricots, dried: 1 pound = 2¾ cups = 4½ to 5½ cups cooked

Asparagus, fresh: 1 pound = 16 to 20 spears

Asparagus, frozen, cut: 1 package (10 ounces) = 2 cups

B

Bananas: 1 pound = 3 to 4 medium = 2 cups sliced = 1¾ cups mashed

Beans, green, fresh: 1 pound = 3½ cups whole

Beans, green, frozen: 1 package (9 ounces) = 1½ cups

Beans, kidney, canned: 16 to 17 ounces = 2 cups

Beans, kidney, dried: 1 pound = 2½ cups = 5½ cups cooked

Beans, navy, dried: 1 pound = 2⅓ cups = 5½ cups cooked

Beef broth: 1 can (14 ounces) = 1¾ cups

Beef, cooked, cubed: 1 cup = 6 ounces

Beef, ground: 1 pound = 2 cups uncooked

Beets, fresh, without tops: 1 pound = 2 cups chopped

Bread: 1 slice fresh = ½ cup soft crumbs = ¼ to ⅓ cup dry crumbs

Broccoli, fresh: 1 pound = 2 cups chopped

Broccoli, frozen: 1 package (10 ounces) = 1½ cups chopped

Brussels sprouts, fresh: 1 pound = 4 cups

C

Cabbage: 1 pound = 3½ to 4½ cups shredded = 2 cups cooked

Carrots, fresh: 1 pound without tops = 3 cups chopped or sliced = 2½ to 3 cups shredded; 1 medium = ½ cup chopped or sliced

135

Carrots, frozen: 1 package (1 pound) = 2½ to 3 cups sliced

Cauliflower: 1 pound = 1½ cups small florets

Celery: 1 stalk (rib) = ½ cup chopped or sliced

Cheese – blue, feta, gorgonzola: 4 ounces = 1 cup crumbled

Cheese – cheddar, Monterey Jack: 1 pound = 4 cups shredded or grated

Cheese – Parmesan, Romano: 4 ounces = 1 cup shredded or grated

Chicken, cooked, cubed: 1 cup = 6 ounces

Chicken broth: 1 can (14 ounces) = 1¾ cups

Corn, fresh: 2 to 3 ears = 1 cup kernels

Corn, frozen: 1 package (10 ounces) = 1¾ cups kernels

Cornmeal: 1 pound dry = 3 cups uncooked = 12 cups cooked

E

Egg, large: 1 yolk = 1 tablespoon; 1 white = 2 tablespoons

Egg, large: 7 to 8 = 1 cup

Eggplant: 1 pound = 3 to 4 cups diced

Egg substitute: ¼ cup = 1 whole egg; 1 package (8 ounces) = 1 cup
= 4 whole eggs

G

Garlic: 2 medium cloves = 1 teaspoon minced

H

Herbs – basil, cilantro, dill, parsley, thyme: 1 tablespoon fresh, chopped
= 1 teaspoon dried

L

Lemon: 1 medium = 2 to 3 teaspoons grated peel and 3 tablespoons juice;
1 pound = 4 to 6 medium lemons = 1 cup juice

Lime: 1 medium = 1 teaspoon grated peel and 2 tablespoons juice;
1 pound = 6 to 8 medium limes = ⅓ to ⅔ cup juice

M

Macaroni: 1 pound = 4 cups dry = 8 cups cooked

Mushrooms, fresh: ½ pound = 2½ to 3 cups sliced = 1 cup sliced, sautéed

N

Noodles: 1 pound = 6 cups dry = 7 cups cooked

O

Okra, fresh: 1 pound = 2 cups sliced

Onion: 1 medium = ½ cup minced = ¾ to 1 cup chopped

Orange: 1 medium = 2 tablespoons grated peel and ⅓ cup juice;
1 pound = 3 medium = 1 cup juice

P

Parsnips: 1 pound = 4 medium = 2 cups chopped

Peas, frozen: 1 package (10 ounces) = 2 cups

Peas, in pod: 1 pound = 1 to 1½ cups shelled

Peppers: 1 medium sweet = 1 cup chopped

Potatoes, sweet: 1 pound = 3 medium = 3½ to 4 cups cubed or sliced = 2 cups mashed

Potatoes, white: 1 pound = 3 medium = 3½ to 4 cups cubed or sliced = 2 cups mashed

R

Rice, brown: 1 cup uncooked = 4 cups cooked

Rice, white: 1 cup uncooked = 3 cups cooked

S

Scallions: 2 medium, white part only = 1 tablespoon; 2 medium including green tops = ¼ cup

Spinach, fresh: 1 pound = 8 to 10 cups torn

Squash, yellow or zucchini: 1 pound = 3 medium = 2½ cups sliced

Squash, winter: 1 pound = 1 cup mashed

T

Tomato: 1 medium = ½ cup chopped; 1 pound = 3 large = 4 medium = 1½ cups chopped

Tomatoes: 1 can (28 ounces) crushed = 3¾ cups

Y

Yogurt: ½ pint = 1 cup = 8 ounces

Culinary Abbreviations

t = **tsp** = teaspoon	**lb** = pound	**mL** = milliliter
T = **tbsp** = tablespoon	**g** = gram	**F** = Fahrenheit
c = cup	**kg** = kilogram	**C** = Celsius
oz = ounce	**mg** = milligram	
fl oz = fluid ounce	**L** = liter	

Index

C

cabbage soup with walnuts, 21
Cajun salmon, 89
capers, 59
Caribbean chicken with parsnips, 49
carrot–fava bean soup with peppers, 22
cauliflower and turkey Tetrazzini, 60
chayote squash, stuffed, 39
cheddar cheese bread, 105
cheeses, grated, 50
cheese-scalloped potatoes, 38
chick peas. *See* garbanzo beans

Chicken:
    chicken with apples and thyme, 47
    chicken breasts, stuffed, 53
    chicken, carrot, and apple stew, 12
    chicken casserole with Swiss cheese, 56
    chicken, curried, 52
    chicken with fennel, 54
    chicken with fruit salsa, 55
    chicken with parsnips, 49
    chicken Parmesan, 50
    chicken soup with zucchini, 35
    chicken stew with mushrooms, 14, 19, 51
    chicken stew with peppers, mushrooms, and squash, 19
    chicken stew with tomatoes, 13
    chicken, stuffed, 48
    chicken with sun-dried tomatoes, 13

Chili:
    chipotle chili, 39
    chili, with garbanzo beans and ham, 66
    chili peppers, preparing, 32, 39, 46, 66

Chili, continued
    chili, pork, 65
    chili-stuffed chayote squash, 39
Chinese beef balls with bok choy, 63
chipotle chilies, 39
chorizo–tortilla soup, 23
chowder, sea scallop, 29
cinnamon–walnut bread, 101

Clay pot:
    cleanup, 7–8
    deodorizing, 8
    doneness, checking, 9
    preparation and care, 5–8
cod fillets with lemon and thyme, 91
cod with tomatoes, 89
compote, 111, 115
converting recipes for clay pot, 9
corn chowder, 25
corned beef with red cabbage, 61
cornmeal substitute, 49
country-style chicken stew Provençal, 14
creamy chicken with roasted peppers, 51
creamy potato soup, 24
crisps (desserts), 109, 113
crystallized ginger, 113
culinary math (chart), 135–137
curried chicken, 52

D

Dairy:
    herbs to use with, 127–130
    spices to use with, 130–132
dark wheat bread, 103
deodorizing pot, 8
desserts, 109–115

E

easy chicken breasts with stuffing, 53
easy pork–chipotle chili, 65